SOLARO STUDY GUIDE—Geography of Canada 9 Academic (CGC1D)

SOLARO Study Guide consists of the following sections:

KeyTips for Being Successful at School gives examples of study and review strategies. It includes information about learning styles, study schedules, and note taking for test preparation.

Class Focus includes a unit on each area of the curriculum. Units are divided into sections, each focusing on one of the specific expectations, or main ideas, that students must learn about in that unit. Examples, definitions, and visuals help to explain each main idea. Practice questions on the main ideas are also included. At the end of each unit is a test on the important ideas covered. The practice questions and unit tests help students identify areas they know and those they need to study more. They can also be used as preparation for tests and quizzes. Most questions are of average difficulty, though some are easy and some are hard—the harder questions are called *Challenger Questions*. Each unit is prefaced by a **Table of Correlations**, which correlates questions in the unit (and in the practice tests at the end of the book) to the specific curriculum expectations. Answers and solutions are found at the end of each unit.

Key Strategies for Success on Tests helps students get ready for tests. It shows students different types of questions they might see, word clues to look for when reading them, and hints for answering them.

Practice Tests includes one to three tests based on the entire course. They are very similar to the format and level of difficulty that students may encounter on final tests. In some regions, these tests may be reprinted versions of official tests, or reflect the same difficulty levels and formats as official versions. This gives students the chance to practice using real-world examples. Answers and complete solutions are provided at the end of the section.

For the complete curriculum document (including specific expectations along with examples and sample problems), visit www.edu.gov.on.ca/eng/curriculum/secondary.

SOLARO Study Guide Study Guides are available for many courses. Check www.castlerockresearch.com for a complete listing of books available for your area.

For information about any of our resources or services, please call Castle Rock Research at 1.800.840.6224 or visit our website at http://www.castlerockresearch.com.

At Castle Rock Research, we strive to produce an error-free resource. If you should find an error, please contact us so that future editions can be corrected.

D1088819

TABLE OF CONTENTS

KEY TIPS FOR BEING SUCCESSFUL AT SCHOOL 1

    Key Factors Contributing to School Success 2

    How to Find Your Learning Style 3

    Scheduling Study Time 4

    Creating Study Notes 5

    Memorization Techniques 7

    Key Strategies for Reviewing 7

    Key Strategies for Success: A Checklist 8

GEOGRAPHIC FOUNDATIONS 9

    Table of Correlations 10

        Terms and Concepts Associated with Regions 11

        Characteristics of Natural Systems 11

        Characteristics of Human Systems 12

        Canadian Ecozones 13

        Characteristics of Urban and Rural Environments 14

        Location of Businesses, Industries, and Transportation Systems 16

        Canada's Population Density 17

        Population Patterns in Canada 19

        Regional Distribution Patterns of Various Peoples Across Canada 19

        Location of Recent First Nation Land Claims in Canada 20

        Evaluating the Effect of Government Land Use Policy on Local Planning 21

        Considerations in Comparing Different Ways of Providing Human Systems:
        for a Territory and Areas of Southern Canada 21

        The Best Place to Live in Canada: Identifying and Justifying Your Choice 22

        Predict Future Locations of Canadian Businesses, Industries, and Transportation Systems 23

        Identify and Describe Examples of Canadian Art Reflecting Natural or Cultural Landscapes 24

    Practice Questions—Geographic Foundations 26

    Answers and Solutions—Practice Questions 32

    Unit Test—Geographic Foundations 36

    Answers and Solutions—Unit Test 42

HUMAN-ENVIRONMENT INTERACTIONS **47**

  Table of Correlations **48**

    Human Activities that Affect the Environment or are Affected by the Environment 49

    How Natural Systems Influence Cultural and Economic Activities 51

    Regional Distribution and Importance of Canada's Energy Sources...52

    The Role of Government in Managing Resources and Protecting the Environment.......................53

    How Traditional Ecological Knowledge of Aboriginal Peoples
    Influences their Interactions with the Environment 53

    Assessing the Value of Canada's Key Natural Resources 54

    Assessing the Feasibility of Using Selected Renewable and Alternative Energy Sources............56

    Evaluating Differing Viewpoints on the Benefits and Disadvantages
    of Selected Resource Megaprojects 57

    The Affects of Urban Growth on the Natural Environment 58

    Researching and Presenting Ways to Improve the Balance Between
    Human and Natural Systems..59

    Analyzing and Evaluating the Success of Local Waste Management Methods 59

    Evaluating Solutions to Environmental Problems Proposed
    by Various Groups and Making Recommendations for Sustainable Resource Use 60

    Quality of Life 61

  Practice Questions—Human-Environment Interactions...**62**

  Answers and Solutions—Practice Questions **64**

  Unit Test—Human-Environment Interactions...**66**

  Answers and Solutions—Unit Test..**69**

GLOBAL CONNECTIONS **71**

  Table of Correlations **72**

    Canadian Participation in International Organizations and Agreements 73

    Canada's Global Contributions..74

    Natural Systems in Canada 75

    Canada's Approaches to Environmental Concerns 76

    Canada's Participation in Global Organizations 78

    The Global Distribution of Selected Commodities..78

    Canada's Economy and the World 79

    Tourism and Canada's Economic Development...80

    Ecological Footprints...80

    Developing a Solution to a Global, Geographic, or Environmental Issue......................................81

  Practice Questions—Global Connections **82**

  Answers and Solutions—Practice Questions **84**

  Unit Test—Global Connections **86**

  Answers and Solutions—Unit Test..**91**

UNDERSTANDING AND MANAGING CHANGE **95**

   Table of Correlations **96**

      Diversity 97

      Change in Human and Natural Systems 97

      Demographics and Migration in Canada 100

      Different Perspectives on Geographic Issues 102

      The Consequences of Human Activities on Natural Systems 103

      Effects of Manufacturing, Transportation, and Consumption of Products ... 104

      Impact of Change on a Planning Project 106

      Global Environmental Changes 107

   Practice Questions—Understanding and Managing Change **109**

   Answers and Solutions—Practice Questions **111**

   Unit Test—Understanding and Managing Change **113**

   Answers and Solutions—Unit Test **116**

METHODS OF HISTORICAL INQUIRY AND COMMUNICATION **119**

      Research 120

      Checking Reliability 121

      Primary and Secondary Sources 122

      Documentation 127

      Formulating Questions 128

      Drawing Conclusions 129

      Analysing Information 130

      Assessing Both Sides of an Issue 133

KEY STRATEGIES FOR SUCCESS ON TESTS **135**

      Test Preparation and Test-Taking Skills 136

      Test Preparation Countdown 139

      Summary of How to be Successful During the Test 140

PRACTICE TEST **141**

   Table of Correlations **142**

   Practice Test **144**

   Answers and Solutions—Practice Test **156**

APPENDICES **165**

      Glossary 166

      Credits 169

Key Tips for being Successful at School

KEY TIPS FOR BEING SUCCESSFUL AT SCHOOL

KEY FACTORS CONTRIBUTING TO SCHOOL SUCCESS

In addition to learning the content of your courses, there are some other things that you can do to help you do your best at school. You can try some of the following strategies:

- **Keep a positive attitude:** Always reflect on what you can already do and what you already know.

- **Be prepared to learn:** Have the necessary pencils, pens, notebooks, and other required materials for participating in class ready.

- **Complete all of your assignments:** Do your best to finish all of your assignments. Even if you know the material well, practice will reinforce your knowledge. If an assignment or question is difficult for you, work through it as far as you can so that your teacher can see exactly where you are having difficulty.

- **Set small goals for yourself when you are learning new material:** For example, when learning the parts of speech, do not try to learn everything in one night. Work on only one part or section each study session. When you have memorized one particular part of speech and understand it, move on to another one. Continue this process until you have memorized and learned all the parts of speech.

- **Review your classroom work regularly at home:** Review to make sure you understand the material you learned in class.

- **Ask your teacher for help:** Your teacher will help you if you do not understand something or if you are having a difficult time completing your assignments.

- **Get plenty of rest and exercise:** Concentrating in class is hard work. It is important to be well-rested and have time to relax and socialize with your friends. This helps you keep a positive attitude about your schoolwork.

- **Eat healthy meals:** A balanced diet keeps you healthy and gives you the energy you need for studying at school and at home.

How to Find Your Learning Style

Every student learns differently. The manner in which you learn best is called your learning style. By knowing your learning style, you can increase your success at school. Most students use a combination of learning styles. Do you know what type of learner you are? Read the following descriptions. Which of these common learning styles do you use most often?

- **Linguistic Learner:** You may learn best by saying, hearing, and seeing words. You are probably really good at memorizing things such as dates, places, names, and facts. You may need to write down the steps in a process, a formula, or the actions that lead up to a significant event, and then say them out loud.

- **Spatial Learner:** You may learn best by looking at and working with pictures. You are probably really good at puzzles, imagining things, and reading maps and charts. You may need to use strategies like mind mapping and webbing to organize your information and study notes.

- **Kinesthetic Learner:** You may learn best by touching, moving, and figuring things out using manipulatives. You are probably really good at physical activities and learning through movement. You may need to draw your finger over a diagram to remember it, tap out the steps needed to solve a problem, or feel yourself writing or typing a formula.

SCHEDULING STUDY TIME

You should review your class notes regularly to ensure that you have a clear understanding of all the new material you learned. Reviewing your lessons on a regular basis helps you to learn and remember ideas and concepts. It also reduces the quantity of material that you need to study prior to a test. Establishing a study schedule will help you to make the best use of your time.

Regardless of the type of study schedule you use, you may want to consider the following suggestions to maximize your study time and effort:

- Organize your work so that you begin with the most challenging material first.
- Divide the subject's content into small, manageable chunks.
- Alternate regularly between your different subjects and types of study activities in order to maintain your interest and motivation.
- Make a daily list with headings like "Must Do," "Should Do," and "Could Do."
- Begin each study session by quickly reviewing what you studied the day before.
- Maintain your usual routine of eating, sleeping, and exercising to help you concentrate better for extended periods of time.

CREATING STUDY NOTES

MIND-MAPPING OR WEBBING

Use the key words, ideas, or concepts from your class notes to create a mind map or web, which is a diagram or visual representation of the given information. A mind map or web is sometimes referred to as a knowledge map. Use the following steps to create a mind map or web:

1. Write the key word, concept, theory, or formula in the centre of your page.
2. Write down related facts, ideas, events, and information, and link them to the central concept with lines.
3. Use coloured markers, underlining, or symbols to emphasize things such as relationships, timelines, and important information.

The following mind map is an example of one that could help you develop an essay:

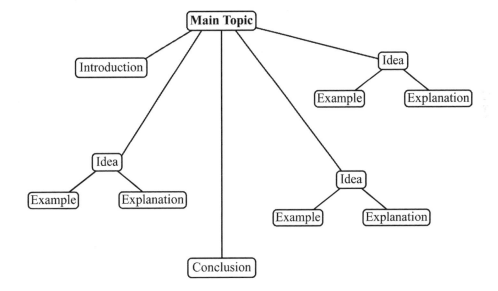

INDEX CARDS

To use index cards while studying, follow these steps:

1. Write a key word or question on one side of an index card.

2. On the reverse side, write the definition of the word, answer to the question, or any other important information that you want to remember.

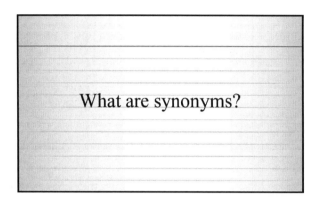

SYMBOLS AND STICKY NOTES—IDENTIFYING IMPORTANT INFORMATION

Use symbols to mark your class notes. The following are some examples:

- An exclamation mark (!) might be used to point out something that must be learned well because it is a very important idea.

- A question mark (?) may highlight something you are not certain about

- A diamond (◊) or asterisk (*) could highlight interesting information that you want to remember.

Sticky notes are useful in the following situations:

- Use sticky notes when you are not allowed to put marks in books.

- Use sticky notes to mark a page in a book that contains an important diagram, formula, explanation, or other information.

- Use sticky notes to mark important facts in research books.

MEMORIZATION TECHNIQUES

- **Association** relates new learning to something you already know. For example, to remember the spelling difference between dessert and desert, recall that the word *sand* has only one *s*. So, because there is sand in a desert, the word *desert* has only one *s*.

- **Mnemonic** devices are sentences that you create to remember a list or group of items. For example, the first letter of each word in the phrase "Every Good Boy Deserves Fudge" helps you to remember the names of the lines on the treble-clef staff (E, G, B, D, and F) in music.

- **Acronyms** are words that are formed from the first letters or parts of the words in a group. For example, RADAR is actually an acronym for Radio Detecting and Ranging, and MASH is an acronym for Mobile Army Surgical Hospital. HOMES helps you to remember the names of the five Great Lakes (Huron, Ontario, Michigan, Erie, and Superior).

- **Visualizing** requires you to use your mind's eye to "see" a chart, list, map, diagram, or sentence as it is in your textbook or notes, on the chalkboard or computer screen, or in a display.

- **Initialisms** are abbreviations that are formed from the first letters or parts of the words in a group. Unlike acronyms, an initialism cannot be pronounced as a word itself. For example, GCF is an initialism for **G**reatest **C**ommon **F**actor.

KEY STRATEGIES FOR REVIEWING

Reviewing textbook material, class notes, and handouts should be an ongoing activity. Spending time reviewing becomes more critical when you are preparing for a test. You may find some of the following review strategies useful when studying during your scheduled study time:

- Before reading a selection, preview it by noting the headings, charts, graphs, and chapter questions.

- Before reviewing a unit, note the headings, charts, graphs, and chapter questions.

- Highlight key concepts, vocabulary, definitions, and formulas.

- Skim the paragraph, and note the key words, phrases, and information.

- Carefully read over each step in a procedure.

- Draw a picture or diagram to help make the concept clearer.

KEY STRATEGIES FOR SUCCESS: A CHECKLIST

Reviewing is a huge part of doing well at school and preparing for tests. Here is a checklist for you to keep track of how many suggested strategies for success you are using. Read each question, and put a check mark (✓) in the correct column. Look at the questions where you have checked the "No" column. Think about how you might try using some of these strategies to help you do your best at school.

Key Strategies for Success	Yes	No
Do you attend school regularly?		
Do you know your personal learning style—how you learn best?		
Do you spend 15 to 30 minutes a day reviewing your notes?		
Do you study in a quiet place at home?		
Do you clearly mark the most important ideas in your study notes?		
Do you use sticky notes to mark texts and research books?		
Do you practise answering multiple-choice and written-response questions?		
Do you ask your teacher for help when you need it?		
Are you maintaining a healthy diet and sleep routine?		
Are you participating in regular physical activity?		

Geographic Foundations

GEOGRAPHIC FOUNDATIONS

Table of Correlations		
Specific Expectation	**Practice Questions**	**Unit Test Questions**
Students are expected to:		
1.1 *describe the components and patterns of Canada's spatial organization*		
1.1.1 explain the terms and concepts associated with regions	1, 2	1, 2
1.1.2 describe the characteristics of natural systems	3, 4	3, 4
1.1.3 describe the characteristics of human systems	5, 6	5, 6
1.1.4 outline the criteria used to define selected Canadian ecozones and describe the processes and interactions that shape those coziness	7, 8	7, 8
1.1.5 distinguish between the characteristics of urban and rural environments	9, 10	9, 10
1.1.6 explain the geographical requirements that determine the location of businesses, industries, and transportation systems	11, 12	11, 12
1.2 *demonstrate an understanding of the regional diversity of Canada's natural and human systems*		
1.2.1 analyse variations in population density and use their findings to explain overall population patterns	13, 14	13, 14
1.2.2 illustrate and explain the regional distribution patterns of various peoples across Canada	15, 16	15, 16
1.2.3 analyse the location pattern of recent First Nation land claims in Canada	17, 18	17, 18
1.3 *analyse local and regional factors that affect Canada's natural and human systems*		
1.3.1 identify criteria with which to evaluate the effect of government land use policy on planning in the local community	19, 20	19
1.3.2 compare different ways of providing human systems for a territory and areas in southern Canada	21	20, 21
1.3.3 use a reasoned argument to identify the best place to live in Canada and justify their choice	22	22
1.3.4 predict future locations of businesses, industries, and transportation systems in Canada	23	23, 24
1.3.5 identify and describe examples of Canadian art that reflect natural or cultural landscapes	24	25

GEOGRAPHIC FOUNDATIONS

1.1.1   explain the following terms and concepts associated with regions

TERMS AND CONCEPTS ASSOCIATED WITH REGIONS

A **bioregion** is a localized area with unique natural characteristics, such as climate, landforms, soils, plants, and animals. Bioregions are small in size and usually form around a common **watershed**, which drains rain or snowfall toward a particular waterway.

An **ecozone** is a vast region comprising a combination of interacting human and natural characteristics. In Canada, there are fifteen terrestrial **ecozones** (land-based) and five marine ecozones (ocean-bordering). Ecozones contain a number of smaller areas called ecosystems, and each ecosystem is a community of animals and plants that interact within their environment. Examples of an ecosystem are a local wetland or a forest.

Boundaries are natural lines, or borders, that separate one region from another. The tree line is an example of a boundary from which latitudes to the north are unsuitable for trees to grow. The area to the north, which is known as tundra, is too dry and cold to support the growth of trees.

The **transition zone** is a boundary through which the features of one **ecozone** gradually blend in a transitional area with characteristics of the next ecozone. Transition zones contain the combined features of the ecozones in the area where one ecozone ends and another starts.

During the mid-1990s, Dr. William Rees developed the idea of the **ecological footprint** to educate people about their own lifestyle choices. It is a measurement in hectares that calculates the amount of land and resources required to support the lifestyle of a country or an individual. Factors used to calculate the footprints include use of transportation, water, and space required for work and living. Canada's footprint of 7.7 hectares is comparatively much higher than the world average of 2.2 hectares. City planners now try to lower the ecological footprint in order to develop sustainable communities.

Geographers refer to any inhabited areas of the world as **ecumenes**. Inhabited areas include the land on which people live and also their work areas that are occupied and used for economic purposes. Many types of ecumenes exist, each with its own characteristics; for example, population ecumenes, industrial ecumenes, and agricultural ecumenes.

1.1.2   describe the characteristics of natural systems

CHARACTERISTICS OF NATURAL SYSTEMS

The natural systems in the environment are complex and interconnected in an unlimited number of ways. Describing a natural system will also inevitably involve the discussion of other natural systems because components of these systems are dependent upon each other.

Climate is the average patterns of weather that have existed in particular regions over many years. Climate affects all living things on Earth. Globally, climate is constantly changing and forms as a result of the atmosphere, differences in landforms that exist on Earth, and the circulation of water throughout the oceans. The key factor in determining the nature of an ecosystem is climate.

Biomes are large ecological regions on Earth that are named after the distinct characteristics of the plants living within them. Grasslands, rainforests, and deserts are all types of biomes. Specific types of plants grow in each biome as a result of the landforms and climate that they interact with in those regions. The largest biome and natural ecosystem on Earth is the boreal forest.

The **lithosphere** is Earth's outer layer. The lithosphere, which is approximately 100 km thick, includes all of Earth's crust and the top part of its mantle. Composed of rock, soil, and minerals, the lithosphere provides a place for living things to exist. Additionally, it provides a place for water to gather that in turn is essential to all life forms.

The **atmosphere** is the thin layer of odourless, colourless, and tasteless gases surrounding Earth. The atmosphere contains the gases necessary to sustain life. Weather systems that influence cycles of life on Earth form in the atmosphere. Sunlight, which enters the atmosphere and heats Earth, is the major source of energy on Earth. For example, plants within biomes use energy from the sun for photosynthesis, which creates chemical energy and utilizes available water from the hydrosphere.

The **hydrosphere** includes all forms of water on Earth's crust (solid, liquid, and gas). The hydrosphere exists in the atmosphere as vapour and clouds. On Earth, water exists in salty and fresh water forms such as ice, oceans, lakes, swamps, groundwater, and the water within animals and plants. Fresh water covers only 3% of Earth's surface. Water is essential to the survival of all living things on Earth.

1.1.3   describe the characteristics of human systems

Characteristics of Human Systems

There are several types of systems in Canadian society. These systems are complex and interconnected networks that support human activities. For example, communication is necessary to the success of virtually all human systems. Like natural systems, human systems display synergy. This means that each of these systems is greatest when it functions as a whole.

Transportation systems are interconnected networks of roads and routes (rail, bus, bicycle, air, and waterways) designed to easily move people and all kinds of goods across Canada. The transportation and economic systems are closely linked because Canadian economy and industries depend upon movement of natural resources and finished products. Transportation systems have played a key role in the settlement and development of Canada.

Communication systems involve all types of communication such as telephone and e-mail networks, advertising, the media, the Internet, and satellites. Communication systems enable places and people to be connected to each other. Thriving communities develop as a result of viable natural resources and highly integrated communication, economic, and transportation systems.

Infrastructure systems are the networks of basic services that communities and economies need in order to function successfully. Much of Canada's extensive infrastructure is built and hidden underground from sight. The infrastructure system of a community provides necessary services such as supplying water and electricity, and it also includes transportation networks.

Energy networks provide the energy necessary to support the Canadian lifestyle. Energy powers homes, industrial activities, and the economy. Energy types include non-renewable natural resources such as fossil fuels and natural gas, and renewable types that include hydro-electricity, solar and tidal power, and wind energy. Energy networks serve to collect, transport, and deliver sources of energy to consumers after they are transformed into useful products such as electricity, gasoline, and steam. A number of energy networks are global in nature. Transportation systems and energy networks are strongly interconnected as different energy fuels require transport to local and distant markets. Natural gas, for example, travels through pipelines.

Economic systems are coordinated and combined activities that enable goods and services to be produced and delivered. As most Canadians work away from their homes, economic systems are closely aligned with transportation systems, thus enabling Canadians to travel to their workplace and, in turn, contribute to the economy of the community that they live in. A dynamic trade system moves products, money, and services across Canada. As well, economic systems serve to link people throughout Canada in common economic activities.

EFFECT OF HUMAN SYSTEMS UPON NATURAL SYSTEMS

Unlike natural systems that have evolved over thousands of years, human systems can develop and change quickly. All human systems constantly interact with and affect natural systems, thus changing Earth's natural surface. As people need natural resources to survive, the environment transforms with people's use of the land. The **sustainability**, or the ability to last into the future, of Canadian ecosystems is a topic of major concern to many people. Human systems often affect natural systems in environmentally harmful ways, such as the creating pollution. Highly profiled environmental concerns such as endangered species and climate change illustrate the impact and effect of human interaction upon natural systems and the need for global solutions.

1.1.4   outline the criteria used to define selected Canadian ecozones and describe the processes and interactions that shape those ecozones

CANADIAN ECOZONES

Ecozones are vast regions that contain a combination of interacting human and natural characteristics, similar throughout the region. Like other ecozones throughout the world, Canadian ecozones are each defined as containing common landforms, natural vegetation, soils, climate, wildlife, and human activities. Since links exist among all of the natural features within an ecozone, each of these regions includes a distinct combination of interacting human and natural systems. Climate, which varies greatly across Canada, is a major determiner of the nature of each ecozone. The type of vegetation that grows in each ecozone is directly related to the distance that the region is located latitudinally from the equator.

Canada contains fifteen terrestrial ecozones and five marine ecozones in total. Each of these regions is geographically unique and distinct from each other. Canadian ecozones are constantly changing as a result of the effects of **physical processes** that occur gradually over time such as erosion and weathering. Additionally, human activities and interactions impact and shape the surface of Canada's ecozones, sometimes irreversibly. This is particularly the case in Canada's southern regions; generally, the more heavily populated an area is, the greater the amount of human activity that can impact the environment in damaging ways.

Canada's largest terrestrial ecozone is the Boreal Shield.

The massive Boreal Shield is mainly covered by dense boreal (northern) coniferous forest and the rugged Canadian Shield. The thin soils and exposed rock of the Canadian Shield resulted from the process of glaciation, which scraped rich soils from the region and deposited them in the Great Lakes, St. Lawrence Lowlands, and prairie regions. Areas of wetland bogs of decayed vegetation called **muskeg** and more than 1 000 lakes are also common natural features within the region.

A unique combination of plants and animals live in the Boreal Shield and are dependent upon a habitat consisting mainly of water and rocky terrain. The area is home to many small and large mammals, plus hundreds of different kinds of birds. The continental climate consists of short, hot summers and long, cold winters. Communities tend to be smaller and more spread out, with local economies based on mining and forestry activities. Construction and tourism are also businesses that exist in the region.

Since there is limited access into northern parts of the Boreal Shield, this region remains relatively preserved. However, scientists and analysts are concerned about many southern areas because logging, road building, and other economic activities have impacted parts of the ecosystem. For example, woodland caribou can no longer survive in southern parts of the Boreal Shield. Many people are concerned that actions in this ecozone, such as current logging practices, may not be sustainable for the future.

1.1.5   distinguish between the characteristics of urban and rural environments

CHARACTERISTICS OF URBAN AND RURAL ENVIRONMENTS

Differences in Population Density—An **urban environment** is a centre of human settlement and activity that, through growth, has acquired a large population density. Large towns and cities are examples of urban environments. Through continued growth and diversified local economies, urban environments can experience great surges in population growth. A **rural environment** exists outside of towns and cities, where the land has a low population density. Much of Canada's sprawling rural landscape is composed of lands that are geographically unsuitable to support population settlement, for example, rocky terrain. Approximately one in five Canadians presently lives in rural environments while urban environments support approximately 80% of the country's population.

Land Use—This is a term that refers to the different places in a community that people live in, attend school, work, shop, and attend recreational activities. Urban land use in Canada can be categorized as follows:

- **Residential lands**—used for living space, for example, neighbourhoods with a variety of dwellings such as apartment buildings

- **Transportation lands**—used for transportation routes that move people and goods from place to place, for example, highways

- **Commercial lands**—used for business activities that provide goods and services to people, for example, a shopping mall

- **Industrial lands**—used to support secondary industries, for example, factories

- **Institutional lands**—used for services provided to communities, for example, schools

- **Open space/recreational lands**—unused and protected lands (for example, a woodland park) and lands used for recreation (for example, a soccer field)

While the quality of life in towns and cities is dependent upon how the land in those areas is used, the growth of urban centres affects our natural environment. Currently, the focus of city planners and geographers has been to make cities sustainable for the future while ensuring a good quality of life for those presently living there. A new design principle known as "new urbanism" has emerged whereby urban centres are being planned to be more compact. Neighbourhoods are designed with homes and businesses placed within walking distance from each other. Planning focuses on serving the needs of the community while protecting both green space and wildlife habitats and preventing urban sprawl from encroaching upon the rural environment.

Forms of Settlement—Settlement in Canada has taken many forms, for instance, hamlets, villages, towns, and small or large cities. Most Canadians and new immigrants live in large urban centres, the majority of which are located in the southern regions of our country. Over time, eight very large population masses known as agglomerations have formed where large and adjacent communities have melded together; for example, the Golden Horseshoe area of southern Ontario and the Calgary-Red Deer-Edmonton corridor of population and economic activity are both considered to be agglomerations.

Development Patterns—The settlement and growth of Canada occurred over the last three centuries in an east to west pattern, from the Atlantic to the Pacific and then up to the far north. A number of factors had to be satisfied for settlement to occur, which included suitable land for building, an appealing climate to live in, fertile soil, direct access to waterways and transportation routes, and abundant natural resources that could support primary or secondary industries. Thus, early Canadian settlers were particularly attracted to areas that held these features such as the Great Lakes-St. Lawrence Lowlands and the British Columbia Lower Mainland. As transportation routes linking our country were built and natural resource bases developed, major urban centres emerged across our country. With the continuing growth of economies within these centres, neighbouring areas of population have built up in order to provide necessary services. As great numbers of urban dwellers work within expanding industries, those locations continue to see population growth.

Types of Employment—The economic growth of our country is powered by employment within our major cities and rural communities. People living in rural environments tend to work in resource-based industries, and communities have commonly been built upon the development of one primary resource. Agriculture, mining, forestry, and fishing are all examples of **primary industries**. Employment in large towns and cities occurs mainly in **secondary industries** (for example, manufacturing) and **tertiary**

(service-based) industries. There is an extensive variety of employment that exists in the service industry; health care and finance are examples of service industries. Additionally, a growing number of Canadians work in **quaternary industries**. These are industries involving the formation of knowledge, technology, and ideas in order to create solutions to problems; scientific research and telecommunications are examples of quaternary industries. Historically, most jobs in Canada were dependent upon primary industries. Today, most Canadians work in tertiary industries that support the communities in which they live.

1.1.6   explain the geographical requirements that determine the location of businesses, industries, and transportation systems

LOCATION OF BUSINESSES, INDUSTRIES, AND TRANSPORTATION SYSTEMS

The location of businesses, industries, and transportation systems is dependent upon specific geographic requirements.

Land—A key factor in determining these locations is the availability of large areas of suitable land on which to build facilities that produce goods (**industries**) and market goods or services (**businesses**). Vast areas of land are also necessary to build the road and rail networks used to **transport** goods across Canada and connect with American transportation systems. In a number of rural areas, the suitability of the land to road-building allowed communities to rise up around a resource-based industry. Some rural areas, though they may contain valuable natural resources, are inaccessible; building roads would be too difficult to accomplish through the local terrain.

Natural Resources—These resources are needed for a number of reasons. For secondary industries, having the necessary raw resources nearby, or easily accessible, is essential in order to save time and

costs in manufacturing. For primary industries, there must be a suitable natural resource available to be acquired through mining, harvesting, fishing, or logging operations. Soils necessary for farming must be fertile in order to grow crops. Additionally, a supply of natural resources is also necessary to meet the physical needs (for food, water, and housing) of the people who work in businesses, industries, and transportation systems.

Waterways—It is desirable for businesses, industries, and transportation networks to be located in close proximity to major waterways for trade purposes, the movement of raw materials and finished products, and to provide the water supply that is necessary during manufacturing. Waterways are viewed as highways for ships, so businesses and industries are often built on inland rivers, or in coastal areas, so as to be close to a desirable point of export for goods. As the United States is Canada's main trading partner, many Canadian businesses, industries, and transportation routes have been built on or in close proximity to the Great Lakes-St. Lawrence Seaway in order to facilitate Canada-US trade.

Climate—A suitable climate is primarily a concern for primary resource-based industries for two reasons. Firstly, agriculture requires a climate with adequate sunshine and precipitation in order for crops to flourish during the growing season. Secondly, much of the extraction, acquisition, or harvesting of resources is done outdoors, and satisfactory weather is desirable for workers' comfort.

*1.2.1   analyse variations in population density and use the findings to explain overall
         population patterns*

CANADA'S POPULATION DENSITY

Population density is a measure of the crowdedness of a given area, for example, that of a country. In other words, the total size of a population within a given geographic area divided by the size of that particular land area equals the population density (crowdedness) of that area.

The population density of Canada is calculated in the following manner:

Canada's population (2006)/Canada's size in km = 3.5 people/km^2.

Thus, there are on average 3 to 4 people per square kilometre living in Canada. This is a very low population density compared to other countries in the world; for example, the United Kingdom has a population density of 246 people/km^2, which is 70 times higher than Canada's population density (based on Statistics Canada's 2006 census).

VARIATIONS IN CANADA'S POPULATION DENSITY

Canada's population density of 3.5 people/km^2 should be considered simply as an average for the entire country. In actuality, the population density of Canada varies greatly across the country and is unevenly distributed. As most Canadians prefer to live in urban areas, the population density is much higher in those areas. For example, both the municipalities of Vancouver and Westmount (on the island of Montreal) have population densities of more than 5 000 people/km^2. They are the areas of highest population density in Canada.

QUICK FACTS ABOUT CANADA'S POPULATION DENSITY (2006)

- Nearly 2 in 3 (67%) Canadians live less than 100 km from the Canada-US border on a strip of land comprising about 4% of Canada's total land area.

- Canada's main population growth from 2001 to 2006 was concentrated in the following four regions: southern parts of British Columbia, Ontario, and Quebec, and the Calgary-Red Deer-Edmonton corridor.

- Sixty-eight percent of Canadians (14.1 million people) now live in six metropolitan areas that each have more than 1 million people: Vancouver, Edmonton (new), Calgary (new), Toronto, Montreal, and Ottawa-Gatineau.

- Canada's territories combined equal more than one-third of Canada's land area. The population of the territories now exceeds 100 000 people.

- The province with the fastest growing population from 2002 to 2006 is Alberta, with a rate of 10.6% (twice the national average).

- Population growth in some provinces (for example, Alberta) and territories is believed to be caused by interprovincial migration, while growth in the population of other provinces (for example, Ontario and British Columbia) is believed to be more the result of international immigration.

- Canada's May 16, 2006 census population was 31 612 897.

The map that follows visually demonstrates Canada's population density:

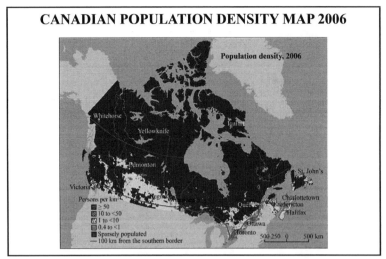

Canada's Population Trend: From Rural to Urban—A steady trend in Canadian population migration, from rural to urban areas, has occurred since the early 1900s. In 1901, 37% of Canada's population lived in urban environments, and therefore 63% of the population lived in rural environments. A little over 100 years later in 2006, 80% of Canadians lived in urban environments and only 20% lived in rural environments. The following chart demonstrates the gradual change in Canada's population from rural-based to urban-based.

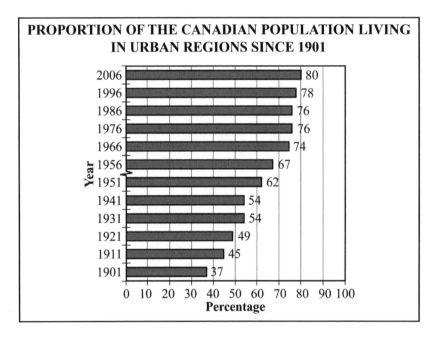

Additionally, of rural environments, only those located within 50 km of urban centres are likely to show population growth (4.7% from 2001 to 2006, which is close to the national average of 5.4%). This is because approximately 30% of the work force in those rural communities commute to work in the nearby urban centres. Remote rural environments that are farther away from large cities showed no population growth from 2001 to 2006.

POPULATION PATTERNS IN CANADA

When variations in Canada's population over time are analysed, several patterns emerge.

Overall, Canada's population has gradually shifted from rural-based to urban-based, mainly because there are fewer employment opportunities linked to primary industries, like agriculture, which are located in rural areas.

Rural areas near large cities show more population growth than remote rural areas because the cities offer employment opportunities that attract people to settle in the nearby smaller communities.

The southern regions of Canada are more heavily populated than other regions due to several factors including historical settlement based on geographic considerations, employment opportunities, and proximity to the United States.

Large urban areas focused on manufacturing attract many people for employment. The majority of Canadians live in one of six large metropolitan areas, primarily for economic reasons.

Growth in some provinces and territories is due to the migration of people between provinces, but in other provinces it is due to international immigration.

1.2.2   illustrate and explain the regional distribution patterns of various people across Canada

REGIONAL DISTRIBUTION PATTERNS OF VARIOUS PEOPLES ACROSS CANADA

Prior to European settlement during the seventeenth century, Canada was inhabited by many Aboriginal communities. The Europeans were the first non-Aboriginal peoples to settle North America. Attracted by the availability of good farmland, abundant natural resources, and waterways, European settlers increasingly moved from eastern to central areas, and finally to western parts of North America. Today, our concentrated southern regions of Canada are extensions of early Canadian settlement as our most populated areas are mainly those that meet the same needs as early European settlers had.

Immigrant Groups—During the twentieth century, immigration from Africa, Asia, and Latin America to Canada increased. Presently, people from many countries throughout the world move to Canada, with the greatest numbers of immigrants coming from countries in Asia. Immigrants, like the majority of Canada's population, often choose to settle in larger population centres because of the employment available in their growing economies. Also, many cultural communities already exist in Canada's major cities. Nearly three-quarters of immigrants that move to Canada settle in the major Canadian cities of Toronto, Montreal, and Vancouver. Well over 40% of immigrants choose to live in Toronto, making it one of the most culturally diverse cities in the world.

Aboriginal Peoples—More than 1 million Aboriginal peoples, who are descendants of Canada's original inhabitants, live in our country, comprising about 5% of our nation's total population. Aboriginal peoples include all **Inuit**, **Métis**, and **First Nations** peoples.

The Inuit make up approximately 5% of Canada's Aboriginal population and live in northern Canada in a region stretching from Labrador to the Northwest Territories. This region is known as Inuit Nunavut, which means "Inuit homeland." Approximately one out of every two Inuit lives in Nunavut.

Approximately 30% of Aboriginal peoples are Métis. The Métis are descendants of Aboriginal peoples and early European fur traders who worked in areas of Canada's western interior. The population of Canada's Métis has nearly doubled since the mid-1990s and is Canada's fastest growing Aboriginal group. Close to 90% of Métis live in the western provinces and Ontario. The majority of the Métis live in urban environments (70%).

First Nations peoples make up the majority of Aboriginal peoples in Canada (over 60%), and there are over 600 First Nations in Canada. Presently, approximately 40% of First Nations peoples live in First Nations communities, formerly called "reserves." These areas of land are owned by the federal government, but have been set aside for use by First Nations through treaties. About 60% of First Nations peoples live away from their Aboriginal home communities, the majority residing in Canada's urban centres. Nearly 85% of Canada's First Nations peoples live in Ontario and the western provinces.

Francophones—Approximately 6 000 000 Francophones make up over 80% of Quebec's population. Francophones living outside of Quebec and throughout Canada make up approximately 5% of Canada's population, the majority living in Ontario. The provinces of Alberta, Ontario, and British Columbia have recorded the highest gains in Francophone population during the last decade. This rise is believed to be due to Francophone migration from other provinces, particularly Quebec, to provinces with growing employment opportunities within their economies.

1.2.3   analyse the location pattern of recent First Nation land claims in Canada

LOCATION OF RECENT FIRST NATION LAND CLAIMS IN CANADA

Many land claims have been pursued by First Nations peoples over the years as they seek to establish legal title to areas of Canada that they live in and/or seek financial compensation for lands given up. This process allows Aboriginal peoples the opportunity to regain some of their lands, their rights, self-governance, and natural resources. It is the responsibility of the federal government to look after Aboriginal land claims, while provincial governments are responsible for property rights.

In recent years, there have two important Aboriginal land claim rulings in Canada. Firstly, in British Columbia in 1997, the Supreme Court of Canada decided that (1) Aboriginal peoples could seek title to lands that they had not given up title to in the past, (2) resource-based industries cannot impact Aboriginal lands, and (3) that Aboriginal peoples could receive compensation for impacted lands. This decision by the Supreme Court, known as Delgamuukw, clearly defined Aboriginal rights in British Columbia.

Secondly, an important ruling by the Supreme Court stated that the federal and provincial governments must consult Aboriginal peoples about land development activities that could impact their rights and potential ownership of lands.

There are two main types of Aboriginal land claims: **specific land claims** and **comprehensive land claims**. Over 200 specific land claims concerning original treaties that have been broken or unfulfilled have been settled. Comprehensive land claims look after Aboriginal claims to land, self-governance, and natural resources in areas where treaties have never existed.

EMERGING PATTERNS

In many areas of Canada, Aboriginal peoples did not surrender their land to the government, and they now seek to claim title to these lands. The given map demonstrates areas of recent comprehensive land claims. Interestingly, areas without treaties tend to encompass land on either the west coast of Canada or eastern parts of Quebec and Labrador. As of 2001, five modern-day treaties and two outstanding (unsettled) claims to land involve large areas in Canada's northern territories. Would these northern lands be valuable? Think of the valuable natural resources that exist in these areas. Regions throughout the interior of Canada are often the topic of specific land claims, as treaties concerning these lands were signed a hundred years ago. Why would interior lands have been signed to treaties long ago? During that time period the government was eager to sign treaties in order to open up the land to settlement.

1.3.1   identify criteria with which to evaluate the effect of government land use policy on planning in the local community

EVALUATING THE EFFECT OF GOVERNMENT LAND USE POLICY ON LOCAL PLANNING

Governments create land use policies in communities in order to provide an urban balance between a prosperous economy and the protection and preservation of both open spaces and wildlife habitats. The criteria, or standard, with which to evaluate the effectiveness of a government in regard to their land use policies is to study whether such a balance does exist. Is there a good quality of life for the citizens of the community? Are natural ecosystems in and surrounding the community protected? The quality of life in a community is strongly affected by decisions that are made about how local lands will be used.

Government land use policies that consider the health and well-being of citizens living in a community to be a priority will plan the location of future industries wisely in order to ensure clean air and the careful management of wastes. For example, pulp and paper mills on average can release up to 150 000 m^3 of wastewater every day. What locations have been chosen for facilities such as these? How close are they located to residential communities, green spaces, and wildlife habitat?

Urban growth affects the environment and natural systems. A major consideration in evaluating land use policy in a community is determining what plans have been implemented to make a community sustainable and that are protective of the local ecosystems. In recent years, local politicians and urban planners have created community plans that address the need for urban development to be sustainable by using resources carefully so that they will last for future generations. Some new design principles, known as "new urbanism" or "smart growth," plan toward more compact communities. Neighborhoods are designed so that homes and services are all within walking distance, thereby limiting the suburban sprawl that often encroaches upon the natural systems of our environment.

1.3.2   compare different ways of providing human systems for a territory and areas in southern Canada

CONSIDERATIONS IN COMPARING DIFFERENT WAYS OF PROVIDING HUMAN SYSTEMS: FOR A TERRITORY AND AREAS OF SOUTHERN CANADA

A comparison of different ways of providing human systems for a territory and areas of southern Canada will likely highlight the greater impact of environmental factors on the provision of human services to northerners. Will geographic factors such as climate and distance from major economic centres cause the delivery of human systems to be different or more specialized in the Arctic region?

Transportation systems are particularly dependent on natural geography; thus, providing transportation in the rural and remote northern regions poses more challenges than in southern regions of Canada. Many roads in the territories are impassible during parts of the year and are subject to change when thawing occurs. Communities are dependent upon air transport for many of their human services. Time can become a major factor in the delivery of services in the North due to distances travelled.

Different forms of telecommunications will be extremely important and necessary in a territory. For example, learning in many classrooms will involve a greater dependency on the Internet. Modern technology provides direct links to classrooms throughout Canada.

Will different levels of government be responsible for different services provided in the territories than they are in southern parts of Canada? Which services usually provided by provincial governments in southern provinces are responsibilities of the federal government in northern territories? How will resource management differ between these two different regions in Canada?

These are some points worth considering in comparing different ways of providing human systems in these two geographically different regions. However, the human systems requirements of people living in either a northern territory or in a southern region of Canada are actually very similar.

What do you feel are different but effective ways to provide human systems for each of these regions' human environments?

_____

_____

_____

_____

_____

_____

_____

_____

1.3.3   use a reasoned argument to identify the best place to live in Canada and justify that choice

THE BEST PLACE TO LIVE IN CANADA: IDENTIFYING AND JUSTIFYING YOUR CHOICE

In order to identify and justify your choice of the best place to live in Canada, you will first need to use and include the geographic concepts you have learned to brainstorm a list of logical possible locations.

Next, you will need to identify, analyse, and evaluate your possible locations in terms of whether they meet the requirements of a number of human and geographic factors, or criteria, that you feel would be important for the most desirable location in Canada to exhibit. For example, is there an abundant supply of natural resources nearby?

Also, remember to consider whether there are any downsides to your possible locations and how this information may play into your decision.

Your final decision will ultimately be a location that you can justify as the most desirable place to live in Canada based on its ability to fulfill your set of human and geographic criteria.

EXAMPLES OF HUMAN AND GEOGRAPHIC CRITERIA TO CONSIDER

• nearby natural resources

• opportunities for employment

• energy sources

• environment suitable to recreational activities

What are other human and geographic criteria to consider?

_____

_____

_____

_____

_____

_____

_____

_____

1.3.4   predict future locations of businesses, industries, and transportation systems in Canada

PREDICT FUTURE LOCATIONS OF CANADIAN BUSINESSES, INDUSTRIES, AND TRANSPORTATION SYSTEMS

Predicting future locations of Canadian businesses, industries, and transportation systems will require the analysis of geographic factors and human systems that are necessary for them to function successfully. With this information, you can create (synthesize) new ideas or solutions that can help you to evaluate your possible locations and then make your prediction(s).

GEOGRAPHIC REQUIREMENTS TO CONSIDER

Future locations will need to have suitable and available areas of land on which to build the necessary structures.

- An abundant supply of natural resources to extract or harvest from the environment (primary industries) or to use in production and manufacturing (secondary industries) will also be necessary.

- Waterways are very important, both as a means of transportation and as a source of energy to be used.

- A suitable climate for many secondary industries is desirable but not a necessity.

- Will a location that is situated on or close to major trading routes be of importance?

HUMAN SYSTEMS REQUIREMENTS

- Energy networks will be necessary to power the businesses, industries, and transportation systems.

- Are there nearby sources of energy?

- An infrastructure system that is already in place or convenient to build will be necessary for services.

- Communication systems will need to be efficient and advanced to make the businesses or industries as profitable as possible. Are quaternary (knowledge-based) industries that can look after solution management and telecommunications necessary?

- Economic systems are required to ensure that goods and services are marketed and delivered appropriately.

- A nearby population base will also be required to work in these ventures.

After analysing these and other factors, where do you predict that future Canadian businesses, industries, and transportation systems will be located?

_____

_____

_____

_____

_____

_____

_____

_____

1.3.5   identify and describe examples of Canadian art that reflect natural or cultural landscapes

IDENTIFY AND DESCRIBE EXAMPLES OF CANADIAN ART REFLECTING NATURAL OR CULTURAL LANDSCAPES

Canada is known as a geographically diverse country that includes a wide variety of spectacular landscapes. Many beautiful cultural and geographic sites exist in Canada. Our country's exceptional natural and cultural landscapes are frequently referred to by Canadian artists in a variety of art forms, for example, dance, drama, literature, music, and visual arts. Many Canadians feel a strong tie to the land and nature and are inspired by Canada's geography and our human interactions within it to express their feelings through the arts.

The diversity of Canada's regions is often featured in expressions of Canada's human and natural features. Some examples are as follows:

- Lush west coast scenery and picturesque areas of central and eastern Canada, often rich in autumn's beautiful colours, have frequently been the focus of landscape paintings.

- Recording artist Susan Aglukark's vibrant songs, which reference Inuit and Aboriginal life, have been widely listened to by many Canadians.

- Superb cultural performances, featuring dancing and singing, are held at folk festivals and multicultural events throughout the country.

- Pictures and recordings about growing up playing hockey and other Canadian pastimes offer a striking recollection of our relationship with the outdoors.

- Canadian writers often weave geographic references into their works; for example, the famous novel *Who Has Seen the Wind* by W.O. Mitchell describes life growing up on the prairies.

- Concern about the sustainability of our natural environment and ecosystems is also expressed by many artists.

- Some artists offer fond recollections of favourite geographic locations, often including descriptions that link human activities to the landscape. This is the case of the following lyrics to the song "On Yonge Street" from Gordon Lightfoot's album *A Painter Passing Through* (1998, Reprise):

See the people walkin' up and down
See the people movin' all around
On the streets of my hometown on Yonge Street
Longest street in the world they say
Summertime soon slips away
I hope I'll see you one fine day on Yonge Street
Everywhere you go in a city by the lake
Back there in the flow you may give a hand a shake
Everyone you pass seems to wanna say hello
Even late at night on the freshly fallen snow

What examples of Canadian art can you locate that reflect Canada's natural or cultural landscapes? Are there messages that the artists include within their works about the environment?

_____

_____

_____

_____

_____

_____

_____

_____

_____

PRACTICE QUESTIONS—GEOGRAPHIC FOUNDATIONS

1. The city of Toronto would **most accurately** be referred to as
    A. a population ecumene
    B. a transition zone
    C. an ecozone
    D. a biome

2. Salmon numbers have been declining in British Columbia. Which of the following factors has **not** contributed to their decline?
    A. Overfishing
    B. Climate change
    C. Dam construction
    D. Habitat destruction

3. Most of the freshwater that makes up the hydrosphere in Canada is found in
    A. oceans
    B. groundwater
    C. lakes and rivers
    D. icebergs and glacial ice

4. What is the **main** difference between a biome and an ecosystem?
    A. Water sources
    B. Location
    C. Climate
    D. Size

5. One example of a renewable energy source is
    A. oil
    B. coal
    C. water
    D. petroleum

6. Polar bears have been greatly affected by climate change in the Arctic and are now an endangered species. The **main** reason polar bears are affected by climate change is that

   A. they cannot survive in any ecosystem other than their own

   B. fish and seals that they eat no longer live throughout the Arctic

   C. their hunting season is shortened by changes in ice break-up and freeze-up

   D. they cannot survive with heavy coats of fur in the warmer Arctic environment

7. Which of the following items would not help define an ecozone?

   A. Water

   B. Logging

   C. Wildlife

   D. Humans

8. In which of the following areas of Canada have ecozones been impacted to the greatest extent by human activity?

   A. Eastern

   B. Western

   C. Northern

   D. Southern

Use the following graph to answer the next two questions.

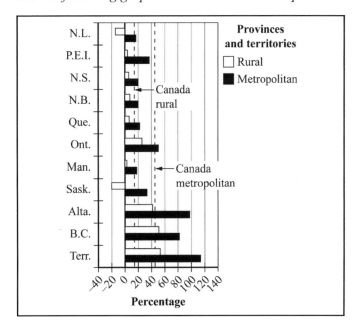

9. Between 1971 and 2001, which of the following provinces had a metropolitan population increase of approximately 50%?

   A. Quebec

   B. Ontario

   C. Manitoba

   D. Prince Edward Island

10. The province that experienced the greatest decrease in rural population between 1971 and 2001 is

    A. Alberta

    B. Ontario

    C. Saskatchewan

    D. Newfoundland

11. One example of a non-renewable resource is

    A. cotton

    B. fertile soil

    C. natural gas

    D. coniferous trees

12. Resource-based communities are those involved with a

    A. primary industry

    B. secondary industry

    C. tertiary industry

    D. quaternary industry

Use the following map to answer the next two questions.

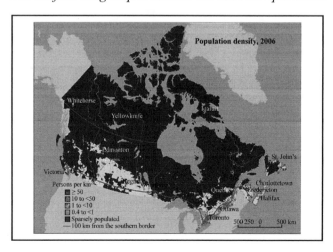

13. Rural population build-up exists outside all of the following cities **except**

    A. Fredericton

    B. Vancouver

    C. Edmonton

    D. Toronto

14. The eastern part of Newfoundland is more populated than other parts of the province **most likely** because

    A. it has a more favourable climate

    B. there is more economic activity in this area

    C. this location provides a direct route to European markets

    D. fishing off the Grand Banks is a large source of employment

15. Which of the following groups of Aboriginals primarily live in the same areas of Canada?

    A. Inuit, Métis, and First Nations

    B. Métis and First Nations

    C. First Nations and Inuit

    D. Inuit and Métis

16. Alberta's greatest source of population increase in recent years has been interprovincial migration. Which of the following reasons for this growth is **false**?

    A. There is no provincial sales tax in Alberta.

    B. Alberta is in the midst of an economic boom.

    C. Agriculture is a major industry in Alberta with many available jobs.

    D. The development of the oil sands has attracted many Canadians to work in Alberta.

17. Which of the following natural resources is least likely to be located in recent Aboriginal land claims areas in Canada?

    A. Oil

    B. Metals

    C. Potash

    D. Diamonds

18. In land claims settlements, financial compensation is sometimes awarded to Aboriginal groups instead of contested lands mainly because

    A. some of the contested lands are now owned by others

    B. the Aboriginal groups prefer the financial compensation

    C. it is hard to divide the lands among Aboriginal communities

    D. the quality of those lands has been affected by erosion over time

19. The development and economic growth of a community most likely environmentally affects which of the following alternatives to the **greatest** extent?

A. citizens

B. homebuyers

C. businesses

D. wildlife

20. Government planning that addresses environmental concerns within communities often tries to provide a balance between the growth of __*i*__ and the protection of __*ii*__ within these communities. This statement is completed **best** by the information in row

Row	*i*	*ii*
A.	animal populations	homeowners' interests
B.	ecosystems	natural habitat
C.	the economy	ecosystems
D.	green space	wildlife

21. Which of the following factors is **least likely** to make the cost of fresh fruit in Nunavut noticeably higher than in other parts of the country?

A. The quality of the fruit

B. The type of transportation used to carry the fruit

C. The amount of time required to transport the fruit

D. The demand within communities for specific food items

22. The majority of Canadians have chosen places to live that are within close proximity to all of the following features **except**

A. major transportation routes

B. the Canada-U.S. border

C. stores and businesses

D. national parks

23. Which of the following types of industry **most likely** operates with the least amount of dependency upon natural resources and labour?

    A. Primary industry

    B. Secondary industry

    C. Tertiary industry

    D. Quaternary industry

24. Which of the following geographic features is commonly captured by artists that paint British Columbia landscapes?

    A. The Appalachians

    B. The Canadian Shield

    C. The Western Cordillera

    D. The Innuitian Mountains

ANSWERS AND SOLUTIONS—PRACTICE QUESTIONS

1. A	7. A	13. A	19. D
2. B	8. D	14. B	20. C
3. D	9. B	15. B	21. A
4. D	10. C	16. C	22. D
5. C	11. C	17. C	23. D
6. C	12. A	18. A	24. C

1. A

The word *ecumene* refers to an inhabited area of the world. An example of a population ecumene is Toronto. A transition zone is a transitional area where the features of one ecozone gradually blend with characteristics of the next ecozone.

An ecozone is an area, usually vast in size, made up of a combination of interacting human and natural characteristics.

Biomes are large ecological areas on Earth that are named after the distinct characteristics of the plants living within them.

2. B

Climate change is not a factor that has contributed to the declining number of salmon. Overfishing by individuals and industries has contributed to declining salmon numbers. Dams have cut off rivers in British Columbia, which has affected the ecosystems in which salmon thrive. Logging, development, and the effects of pollution have all contributed to the decline in salmon numbers in British Columbia.

3. D

Icebergs and glacial ice make up the majority of the freshwater in our hydrosphere. Water is a necessary substance required to sustain all life forms, yet only 2.5 percent of water on Earth is considered freshwater. Two-thirds of that water is frozen in glaciers and ice caps. Much of Canada's north is covered in glacial ice and icebergs. Oceans do not contain freshwater. Groundwater does not make up the majority of the hydrosphere in Canada. Lakes and rivers do not make up the majority of the freshwater in Canada's hydrosphere.

4. D

The main difference is size. A biome is a large area with similar vegetation, wildlife, and microorganisms. Ecosystems are smaller, dynamic systems of plants, animals, and microorganisms working together to create balance. A biome can have many ecosystems within it. Both biomes and ecosystems have the same water sources. Ecosystems are located within biomes; location is not what distinguishes them. Ecosystems and biomes can have the same climate. Thus, climate is not the main difference.

5. C

Water is a renewable resource. A renewable resource is one that either will not run out or can be regenerated within a lifetime. Water, wind, sun, plants, trees, and soil are considered renewable resources. Oil is a non-renewable resource. Coal is a non-renewable resource. Petroleum is a non-renewable resource.

6. C

Polar bears are deprived of a long hunting season because of the early break-up of melting ice and the late freeze-up of ice, which, in turn, are caused by the increase of greenhouse gases in our atmosphere. The question addresses the ecosystem in which polar bears live and not other ecosystems in which they may or may not survive. Fish and seals continue to live in Arctic regions. The current greatest challenge to the survival of polar bears is the diminishing length of their hunting season rather than the thickness of their fur.

7. A

Water is a natural characteristic of ecozones. Logging is an activity, not part of the criteria used to define an ecozone. Wildlife is a natural characteristic of ecozones. Humans form part of the criteria that combine with the natural characteristics of an area to create an ecozone.

8. D

The more populated an area, the greater the amount of human activity that can impact the environment in damaging ways. The majority of Canada's population is in Canada's southern regions. The population of eastern Canada is lower than in southern areas; thus, less human activity has impacted the environment there.

The population of western Canada is lower than in southern areas; thus, less human activity has impacted the environment there. Fewer Canadians live in Canada's northern areas. Not as much human activity that impacts the environment has occurred in these northern areas.

9. B

Ontario experienced an increase in its metropolitan population of approximately 50% during the given time period. Quebec experienced an increase in its metropolitan population of just over 20% during the given time period. Manitoba experienced an increase in its metropolitan population of just over 15% during the given time period. Prince Edward Island experienced an increase in its metropolitan population of nearly 40% during the given time period.

10. C

Saskatchewan experienced the greatest decrease in its rural population (–20%) during the given time period. Alberta did not experience the greatest decrease in rural population during the given time period; in fact, it experienced an increase. Ontario did not experience the greatest decrease in rural population during the given time period; in fact, it experienced an increase. Newfoundland did not experience the greatest decrease in rural population during the given time period; its decrease was less than that of Saskatchewan.

11. C

Natural gas is a non-renewable resource. A non-renewable resource is present in limited supplies and is depleted by use. Natural gas, coal, and oil are all considered non-renewable resources because they took millions of years to form from the buried remains of plants and animals. Cotton is a renewable resource. Cotton is a plant product used to make fabric. Fertile soils can be replenished. Thus, they are a renewable resource. Coniferous trees are a renewable resource.

12. A

Primary industries are resource-based industries in which a resource is harvested or derived from the environment. Farming, logging, and fishing are all examples of resource-based industries. Secondary industries take raw resources and make products from them; i.e., they are manufacturing industries. Tertiary industries are those that provide a service to the community. Quaternary industries are involved with the creation of knowledge, technology, and ideas.

13. A

The map does not indicate a build-up of population outside the city of Fredericton. Because of its smaller size, Fredericton most likely would not have as many employment opportunities as in the larger given cities. Thus, its neighbouring rural population would not have built up because of jobs in the city.

The map indicates that a rural population has built up outside the city of Vancouver. The map indicates that a rural population has built up outside the city of Edmonton. The map indicates that a rural population has built up outside the city of Toronto.

14. B

St. John's location in the eastern part of Newfoundland attracts people to the city to work in its businesses and industries. There is a greater amount of economic activity in the area. The climate is not necessarily more favourable in eastern parts of Newfoundland. This alone would not be a factor to attract a larger population base. The United States is Canada's major trading partner. Therefore, the population in the eastern part of the province would not be larger because of being closer to European markets. The fishing activity in the Grand Banks region has decreased.

15. B

The majority of Métis and First Nations people live in Ontario and the western provinces. The majority of Inuit live throughout the Arctic regions of Canada, whereas the majority of First Nations and Métis people do not. The majority of Inuit live throughout the Arctic regions of Canada, whereas the majority of First Nations people do not. The majority of Inuit live throughout the Arctic regions of Canada, whereas the majority of Métis do not.

16. C

Fewer people are working in the agricultural industry in Alberta; many farms are highly mechanized, employing smaller numbers of workers. There is no provincial sales tax in Alberta, which is attractive to many Canadians. Alberta has experienced an economic boom in recent years. The development of the Alberta oil sands has attracted many workers from out of province.

17. C

Potash is the least likely to be found on lands involved in recent Aboriginal land claims in Canada. Potash is primarily found in Saskatchewan, where there have been fewer land claims. Oil is found in areas involved in recent Aboriginal land claims. Metals, including silver, nickel, and copper, are found in areas involved in recent Aboriginal land claims. Diamonds are found in areas involved in recent Aboriginal land claims.

18. A

Some of the lands are now owned by others. As a result, financial compensation must be negotiated with Aboriginal groups. Aboriginal groups share a very close connection to their land and live in harmony with their natural environment. Being awarded their lands would be of great importance to their identity, culture, and way of life. Issues involving the protection or division of Aboriginal lands would likely not prevent these lands from being awarded to an Aboriginal group.

It would take a great number of years for the quality of those lands to be affected by erosion.

19. D

Wildlife habitats in a community would most likely be affected to a much greater extent by development and economic growth within a community. Economic growth within a community often entails a greater use of community lands, which in turn, can affect our natural systems adversely as wildlife lose the natural habitat of the ecosystems in which they live. Citizens in a community would most likely not be environmentally affected by development and economic growth to the extent that wildlife would be. Homebuyers in a community would most likely not be environmentally affected by development and economic growth to the extent that wildlife would be. Businesses in a community would most likely not be environmentally affected by development and economic growth to the extent that wildlife would be.

20. C

Environmentally conscious governments try
to provide a balance between the growth of a
prosperous economy and the preservation of
ecosystems within their communities. It is unlikely
that environmentally conscious governments
would try to create a balance between the
growth of animal populations and the protection
of homeowners' interests. They likely would
not want the animal populations to increase, or
grow. Ecosystems already are made up of natural
habitats. The balance between an ecosystem and
its natural habitats is not something controlled
by governments. Greater amounts of green
space in a community lead to the preservation
of wildlife habitat. There is no need to have a
balance between the two; wildlife benefit from
as much green space as possibly can be set aside
environmentally.

21. A

The quality of the fruit would be the factor least
likely to make it more expensive than the same
fruit sold in other parts of the country. Much of
the food and supplies that are sold in Nunavut are
transported by plane as a result of the geography of
the region. Plane transportation is very costly. The
amount of time spent transporting goods, especially
perishable food such as fruit, increases their price
because of added labour and refrigeration costs.
There is a lower population in Nunavut. If demand
for particular foods is not high, that food will cost
more to bring in. Fewer people will be buying it,
but the transportation costs will be the same.

22. D

Most national parks are located in rural areas, while
the majority of Canadians live in our major cities.
The majority of Canadians live in urban centres, all
of which are located within major transportation
networks. Nearly 2 in 3 Canadians live within
100 kilometres of the Canada-U.S. border. The
majority of Canadians live in urban centres, all of
which have access to stores and businesses.

23. D

Quaternary industries are concerned with
the formation of knowledge, technology, and
ideas in order to create solutions to problems.
Quaternary industries involve research and
telecommunications, and, as such, are not as reliant
upon labour or natural resources as the other
industries. Primary industries are dependent upon
harvesting natural resources from the environment.
Secondary industries require a large supply
of labour and natural resources from which to
manufacture products. Tertiary industries, which
provide services to people, employ the largest
labour force of any industry.

24. C

The tall and enormous Rockies of the
Western Cordillera are a common subject of
artists that paint British Columbian landscapes.
The Appalachians are located in eastern Canada.
The Canadian Shield is located in central Canada,
not in British Columbia. The Innuitian Mountains
are located in the Arctic.

UNIT TEST—GEOGRAPHIC FOUNDATIONS

Use the following information to answer the next question.

> Take only pictures; leave only footprints.

1. The writer of this statement would **most likely** approve of which of the following human activities?
   A. Preserving our ecosystems
   B. Relocating wildlife habitats
   C. Creating urban sprawl
   D. Building golf courses

2. Which of the following phrases **most accurately** defines the term sustainability?
   A. Taking responsibility for protecting Canada's natural resources
   B. Closely monitoring the effect of human systems on the environment
   C. Using Earth's resources to the greatest possible advantage to gain a profit
   D. Meeting the needs of today's society without reducing the quality of life for future generations

3. All of the components of water on Earth are found in the
   A. biomes
   B. lithosphere
   C. atmosphere
   D. hydrosphere

4. Which of the following scientists interprets radar and satellite imagery in order to make geographic predictions?
   A. Biologist
   B. Ecologist
   C. Volcanologist
   D. Meteorologist

5. An example of a non-renewable natural resource used to generate electricity is
   A. coal
   B. wind
   C. trees
   D. water

6. Our communities depend upon important services that supply electricity, water, heat, roads, and telephones. The given services are **most accurately** referred to as part of a community's

   A. technology

   B. infrastructure

   C. economic system

   D. transportation system

7. Which of the following Canadian ecozones is the **most** physically diverse?

   A. Prairie

   B. Boreal Shield

   C. Mixedwood Plains

   D. Montane Cordillera

8. The unique physical features of the Niagara Escarpment are caused **mainly** by

   A. rising plates on Earth's crust

   B. flow of the Niagara river

   C. glacial movement

   D. erosion

Use the following graph to answer the next question.

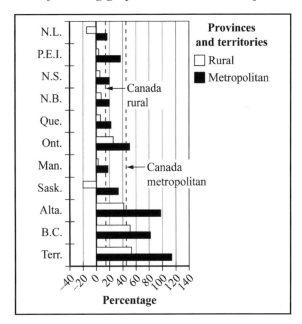

9. Which of the following provinces was likely affected the most by interprovincial migration and international immigration between 1971 and 2001?

   A. Prince Edward Island

   B. New Brunswick

   C. Alberta

   D. Quebec

10. Which of the following factors was **least likely** to have influenced early settlers to live in particular areas?

    A. Waterways

    B. Fossil fuels

    C. Flat lands

    D. Climate

Use the following information to answer the next question.

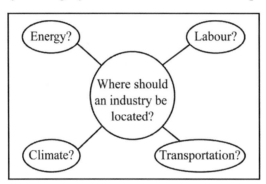

11. Which of the given factors would likely be of **least** importance in deciding upon the location for a furniture factory?

    A. Energy

    B. Labour

    C. Climate

    D. Transportation

12. Most of the grain and natural resources that are harvested and derived from our environment are transported to major centres across Canada by

    A. ship

    B. truck

    C. train

    D. plane

Use the following map to answer the next two questions.

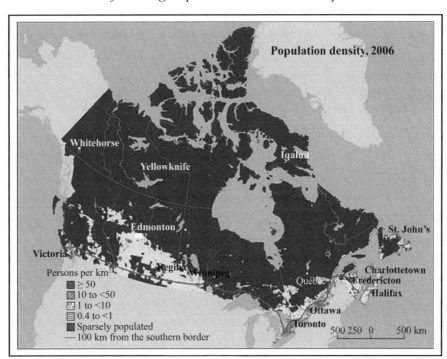

13. Which of the following cities is not located within 100 kilometres of the Canada-U.S. border?

    A. Ottawa

    B. Winnipeg

    C. Vancouver

    D. Charlottetown

14. According to the given map, which of the following cities has the lowest population?

    A. Quebec City

    B. Vancouver

    C. Edmonton

    D. Regina

15. In the past decade, what type of motivation has **most likely** led to an increase in the number of Francophones moving to Alberta and British Columbia?

    A. Cultural

    B. Political

    C. Economic

    D. Educational

16. Which of the following statements about where the majority of immigrants to Canada choose to live and work is **false**?

    A. The majority of immigrants choose to live in Canada's three largest cities.

    B. The majority of immigrants choose to work in primary industries within Canada.

    C. The majority of immigrants choose to live within 100 kilometres of the Canada-U.S. border.

    D. The majority of immigrants choose to work in urban centres in Canada.

17. Which of the following political areas of Canada was formed as a result of a comprehensive land claim settlement affecting its Aboriginal population?

    A. Yukon

    B. Nunavut

    C. Newfoundland

    D. British Columbia

18. Most recent Aboriginal land claims have been settled in which of the following areas of Canada?

    A. Arctic

    B. Pacific Coast

    C. Atlantic Canada

    D. Great Lakes-St. Lawrence Lowlands

19. Which of the following urban planning initiatives is **least likely** for a community seeking to make itself more sustainable for the future?

    A. Design the location of businesses to be within walking distance of homes.

    B. Create more roadways to move traffic more quickly and efficiently.

    C. Provide an assortment of transportation choices.

    D. Protect farmland and woodlots.

20. Which of the following regions would be **most** dependent upon the Internet to provide educational programs to students living there?

    A. Arctic correspondence

    B. Atlantic Canada

    C. British Columbia's Lower Mainland

    D. Golden Horseshoe area of southern Ontario

21. Which of the following services available in Nunavut would be impacted the **least** by the unique nature of the geographic environment there?

    A. Telecommunication service

    B. Infrastructure services

    C. Recreational services

    D. Mail service

22. Which of the following factors is likely of **greatest** significance to immigrants choosing where to live in Canada?

    A. Climate

    B. Employment

    C. Green spaces

    D. Manufacturing

23. Which of the following factors is least likely to be necessary in order to build businesses and industries in a location?

    A. Suitable land

    B. A supply of labour

    C. An appealing climate

    D. Access to natural resources

24. In which of the following locations is a transportation system **least likely** to be built in the future?

    A. Close to cities

    B. In central Alberta

    C. Throughout the Hudson Bay Lowlands

    D. Near natural resources used by industries

Use the following information to answer the next question.

In her famous song, "Big Yellow Taxi," Joni Mitchell sings about paradise being paved in order to build a parking lot.

25. All of the following environmental concerns are touched on by Joni Mitchell in the given example **except**

    A. urban sprawl

    B. global warming

    C. danger to ecosystems

    D. sustainability of our communities

ANSWERS AND SOLUTIONS—UNIT TEST

1. A	8. D	15. C	22. B
2. D	9. C	16. B	23. C
3. D	10. B	17. B	24. C
4. D	11. C	18. A	25. B
5. A	12. C	19. B	
6. B	13. D	20. A	
7. D	14. D	21. A	

1. A

Preserving Earth's ecosystems ensures that natural resources and wildlife are maintained and protected for continued survival. Wildlife habitats are difficult to move as the balance within their fragile ecosystems is easily disrupted. Urban sprawl encroaches upon the environment. Building golf courses is a source of environmentalist concern because golf courses take away the natural habitat of animals.

2. D

The term *sustainability* means meeting the needs of our society without reducing the quality of life for future generations. Taking responsibility for protecting Canada's natural resources does not define the term *sustainability*.

Closely monitoring the effect of human systems on the environment does not define the term *sustainability*. Making communities sustainable for the future would not involve exploiting Earth's natural resources.

3. D

The hydrosphere includes all forms of water on Earth's crust (solid, liquid, and gas). Biomes are large ecological areas on Earth named after the distinct characteristics of plants living within them. The lithosphere is Earth's outer layer. This includes all of Earth's crust and the top part of its mantle. The atmosphere is the thin layer of gases that surround Earth.

4. D

A meteorologist studies the weather and tries to offer predictions. The techniques used include interpreting radar and satellite imagery. A biologist studies humans, plants, animals, and the environments in which they live.

An ecologist studies interactions between organisms and their environment. Ecology is a branch of biology. A volcanologist studies volcanoes, lava, magma, and other related geological phenomena.

5. A

Coal is a non-renewable resource. Wind is a renewable resource. Trees are renewable resources. Water is a renewable resource.

6. B

Infrastructure is the network of basic services that communities depend upon. Most infrastructure exists below Earth's surface. Technology is the practical application of knowledge. It is not specifically a human system on its own but is an important part of all current human systems. Economic systems are combined activities that allow goods and services to be produced, delivered, and used. Transportation systems are interconnected networks of roads and routes.

7. D

The Montane Cordillera is the most physically diverse ecozone, containing a number of differences in vegetation and landform features, such as mountains, valleys, and plateaus. The Prairie ecozone contains primarily flat lands.

The Boreal Shield is a vast area of primarily dense forests. The Mixedwood Plains is Canada's smallest ecozone and contains primarily lowland areas.

8. D

Erosion is responsible for the unique features of the Niagara Escarpment. Lower layers of sandstone and shale are softer than the Escarpment's top, a thick layer of dolomite limestone. Thus, the softer layers have eroded inward at a faster rate and formed the Escarpment's unique physical features.

Rising plates on Earth's crust are not responsible for the Niagara Escarpment's unique physical features. Flow of the Niagara River is not the main cause of the Niagara Escarpment's unique physical features. Glaciers were responsible for leaving thin layers of gravel and sand on top of the Niagara Escarpment's sedimentary rock layers. They are not the main cause of the Escarpment's unique physical features.

9. C

Of the given alternatives, Alberta experienced the greatest increase in urban population (nearly 100%) during the time period. Large increases in urban population are linked to interprovincial migration and international immigration; thus, Alberta was most likely affected the most by these sources of population growth. Prince Edward Island had an increase in its urban population of less than 40% during the given time period. The province was likely not as greatly affected by interprovincial migration and international immigration as Alberta. New Brunswick had an increase in its urban population of approximately 20% during the given time period. The province was likely not as greatly affected by interprovincial migration and international immigration as Alberta. Quebec had an increase in its urban population of just over 20% during the given time period. The province was likely not as greatly affected by interprovincial migration and international immigration as Alberta.

10. B

Fossil fuels are natural resources that are burned as energy sources. Early settlers did not depend on fossil fuels. Instead, they depended upon fire for heat and cooking, wind for sailing, and animals for transportation. Waterways were an important factor that influenced early settlement. Waterways were needed for fresh drinking water and as transportation routes for early settlers. Flat lands were an important factor that influenced early settlement because they are more suitable for building. A suitable, liveable climate was an important factor that influenced early settlement.

11. C

Climate would not be as significant in determining the location of a furniture factory as the work mainly would be done indoors. It would be important to know whether the factory would require large quantities of energy and if energy sources were available. It would be important to know whether the factory would require a large supply of labour. It would be important to determine if the transportation of raw resources or finished products would be expensive or difficult.

12. C

Most of the grain and natural resources that are harvested and derived from our environment are transported by train. There are a variety of train routes across Canada and train transport is more economical. Grain and natural resources are not transported across Canada by ship. Far too much grain is produced in Canada to be transported by truck. It would be far too expensive to transport the bulk of Canada's grain and natural resources by plane.

13. D

The map indicates that Charlottetown is not located within 100 kilometres of the Canada-U.S. border. Charlottetown is located on the island province of Prince Edward Island, a much greater distance than 100 kilometres from the Canada-U.S. border. The map indicates that Ottawa is located within 100 kilometres of the Canada-U.S. border. The map indicates that Winnipeg is located within 100 kilometres of the Canada-U.S. border. The map indicates that Vancouver is located within 100 kilometres of the Canada-U.S. border.

14. D

The map indicates that Regina's population is less than that of the other given cities. The map indicates that Quebec City's population is greater than that of Regina. The map indicates that Vancouver's population is greater than that of Regina. The map indicates that Edmonton's population is greater than that of Regina.

15. C

Like other Canadians, numbers of Francophones have moved to Alberta and British Columbia in search of employment opportunities. The development of industries in Alberta and British Columbia has attracted many workers from out of province, including Francophones. It is unlikely that Francophones have moved to Alberta and British Columbia primarily for cultural reasons as each province does not have an unusually large Francophone population.

It is unlikely that Francophones have moved to Alberta and British Columbia primarily for political reasons. It is unlikely that Francophones have moved to Alberta and British Columbia primarily for educational reasons.

16. B

The majority of immigrants live in Canada's largest cities. Primary industries, however, are located in rural environments where natural resources are harvested. Those who work in primary industries tend to live in rural communities. The majority of immigrants choose to live in Toronto, Montreal, and Vancouver, which are Canada's three largest cities. The majority of immigrants choose to live in Canada's three largest cities, which are all located within 100 kilometres of the Canada-U.S. border. The majority of immigrants choose to work in the urban centres where they live.

17. B

When the Nunavut Land Claims Agreement was signed in 1999, legislation was passed leading to the creation of the new territory of Nunavut. The Yukon Territory was not created as a result of a comprehensive land claim settlement. Newfoundland was not created as a result of a comprehensive land claim settlement. British Columbia was not created as a result of a comprehensive land claim settlement.

18. A

Most recent Aboriginal land claim settlements have taken place in Arctic regions of Canada. Most recent Aboriginal land claim settlements have not taken place in Canada's Pacific Coast area. Most recent Aboriginal land claim settlements have not taken place in Atlantic Canada. Most recent Aboriginal land claim settlements have not taken place in the Great Lakes-St. Lawrence Lowlands area.

19. B

Creating more roadways would be the least likely of the given initiatives to promote sustainability. Roads use up land and promote the use of the automobile as a means of transportation. New initiatives seeking to build sustainability within communities focus on building more walking and bicycle paths, and offering more options for public transportation. New design principles in community planning, referred to as new urbanism or smart growth, seek to mix the use of lands. Businesses and homes are designed to be within walking distance so as to conserve the community and reduce urban sprawl. An assortment of transportation choices gives the population of a community more opportunities to use public transportation, thus cutting down on pollution and emissions within our environment. Protecting farmland, green spaces, and ecologically sensitive lands, such as woodlots and wetlands, helps to promote sustainability of communities and their surrounding natural habitats.

20. A

Many communities in the Arctic region are small and isolated from each other. Arctic communities can utilize telecommunications, such as the Internet, to provide educational programs and resources that would not be available to students in the community otherwise. Students living in Atlantic Canada would most likely not be as dependent upon telecommunications to provide their educational needs as students living in the Arctic. Students living in British Columbia's Lower Mainland would most likely not be as dependent upon telecommunications to provide their educational needs as students living in the Arctic. Students living in the Golden Horseshoe area of southern Ontario would most likely not be as dependent upon telecommunications to provide their educational needs as students living in the Arctic.

21. A

Telecommunications in Nunavut, such as the radio, TV, or Internet, must use satellites. Though costly, satellite service is not as likely to be impacted by the unique geography and remoteness of the region. Geographic factors in Nunavut would influence the amount of time needed to receive infrastructure services, such as the delivery of fresh drinking water or the removal of sewage. Climate and geography influence the type of recreational activities and services that are possible in the outdoor environment of Nunavut. The amount of time to transport the mail in Nunavut would be impacted by geographic factors.

22. B

Among the given factors, employment would most likely be of greatest significance to immigrants new to Canada. Employment would be necessary in order to provide for their need of housing, food, and basic necessities. An appealing climate would probably be desirable but not necessarily the most significant of the given factors. Green spaces would probably be desirable but not necessarily the most significant of the given factors. Many Canadians work in manufacturing in our major cities. Immigrants new to the country would probably be most interested in employment in general, not necessarily employment specifically in the manufacturing industries.

23. C

An appealing climate is not a necessity for many industries in which work is carried out indoors. Suitable land on which to build businesses and industries is necessary. A supply of labour is necessary to fill job positions in businesses and industries. Access to natural resources is necessary in order to have raw materials with which to manufacture and to serve as an energy source.

24. C

The Hudson Bay Lowlands is a marshy area. As a result of poor drainage, much of the land is wet and boggy, unsuitable for building roads. Future transportation systems will more likely be built sooner in the other given areas.

Approximately 80% of Canada's population lives in urban centres. Thus, it is likely that transportation systems will be built to support growing cities with emerging economies. Central Alberta now contains one of Canada's four main population growth regions (the Calgary-Red Deer-Edmonton corridor). As well, there is much economic activity near Alberta's oil sands, to the north of Edmonton. Thus, it is likely that some future transportation systems will be built in central Alberta to accommodate the growing population base and economic activity of the area. Transportation systems will be built near natural resources that industries are dependent upon.

25. B

The environmental issue of global warming is not alluded to in the given example. The environmental issue of urban sprawl is expressed. Present urban planning tries to develop more compact communities that limit urban sprawl, and the use of automobiles and parking lots. Danger to fragile ecosystems is an environmental concern touched on in the given example. Part of an ecosystem has been removed in order to build the parking lot. The environmental issue of sustainability of our communities is brought up in the given example. The parts of paradise that are paved can no longer be passed on to future generations.

HUMAN-ENVIRONMENT INTERACTIONS

Table of Correlations		
Specific Expectation	**Practice Questions**	**Unit Test Questions**
Students are expected to:		
2.1 *explain the relationship of Canada's renewable and non-renewable resources to the Canadian economy*		
2.1.1 explain how human activities affect, or are affected by the environment	1	1, 2
2.1.2 describe how natural systems influence cultural and economic activities	2	3, 4
2.1.3 describe the regional distribution of Canada's energy sources and the relative importance of each source	3	5, 6
2.1.4 identify the role of government in managing resources and protecting the environment	4	7, 8
2.1.5 explain the ways in which the traditional ecological knowledge of Aboriginal peoples, including their concepts of place, wilderness, and boundaries, influences how they interact with their environment	5	9, 10
2.2 *analyse the ways in which natural systems interact with human systems and make predictions about the outcomes of these interactions*		
2.2.1 assess the value of Canada's key natural resources, including agricultural lands and wilderness	6	11, 12
2.2.2 assess the feasibility of using selected renewable and alternative energy sources to implement conservation strategies	7	
2.2.3 evaluate differing viewpoints on the benefits and disadvantages of selected resource megaprojects	8	
2.2.5 present findings from research on ways of improving the balance between human and natural systems	9	
2.3 *evaluate various ways of ensuring resource sustainability in Canada*		
2.3.3 recommend ways in which individuals can contribute to the quality of life in their home, local econzone, province, nation, and the world	10	

HUMAN-ENVIRONMENT INTERACTIONS

2.1.1   explain how human activities affect or are affected by the environment

HUMAN ACTIVITIES THAT AFFECT THE ENVIRONMENT OR ARE AFFECTED BY THE ENVIRONMENT

Human activities and actions can affect the environment by modifying or changing, and in some cases eliminating, the natural systems that exist within it. With the settlement of people and the development of economic activities in a given area, Earth's crust is changed as the natural vegetation and habitat of the area is removed. In Canada, measures have been taken to protect the environment and ecosystems within it where human interactions take place. Protection of the natural systems occurs through the management and conservation of Canada's natural resources. As a result, prime farmland, freshwater sources, and the balance of the ecosystems can be preserved.

AGRICULTURAL AND URBAN DEVELOPMENT

The effect of urban development on agricultural lands is presently a concern for a number of Canadians. Many politicians, environmentalists, and city planners seek to find ways of reducing **urban sprawl**, which occurs as a result of the outward expansion and development of urban areas to nearby bordering areas, including those with valuable farmland. Outlying areas with valuable soils for agriculture are often used for development instead. The land is often too expensive to use for agriculture, and economic activity and urban sprawl often spread out to these areas, cutting the land into smaller parcels that are too minute to sustain economic profitability. Notably, Canada's largest communities exist in areas that contain Canada's best farmland, which is where much of Canada's economic activity occurs. This is primarily a result of early settlement patterns. The Golden Horseshoe area of southern Ontario, which is located in the Mixedwood Plains ecozone, is Canada's largest manufacturing and industrial area. In addressing the region's increasing population and development, the government has taken steps to protect the environment by establishing greenbelt areas around cities in the region, thus limiting urban sprawl.

WASTE MANAGEMENT

Policies concerning waste management exist in Canada as a response to the amount of waste produced by the growing populations and expanding economic activities. One of the main goals of waste management is to provide services that impact the natural systems within ecozones as little as possible. Composting and recycling programs exist in communities across the country. In Ontario, the blue box recycling program became a superb model of an effective environmental initiative, and it has been incorporated in communities throughout North America. Recycled materials acquired through waste management serve to further reduce the needs of people and industries to use more valuable resources.

PARKS DEVELOPMENT

Canada's national and provincial parks serve to protect the country's natural spaces. In order to preserve the natural habitat of Canada's ecozones, areas of rural wilderness have been set aside for protection and conservation. For example, Wood Buffalo National Park, the largest national park in Canada, is also one of the largest protected parks in the world. Established in 1922, it protects some of the last remaining bison herds in Northern Canada while also preserving a large ecological landscape that serves as a representation of Canada's boreal coniferous forests. Also in Canada, wildlife sanctuaries, ecological reserves, and World Heritage Sites seek to safeguard the environment's precious natural systems and areas of wildlife habitat. By protecting the ecological viability of natural spaces in the country, these lands can be enjoyed and appreciated by Canadians today while also being sustainable for future generations.

FOREST HARVESTING

Forests are unique natural systems that are home to a rich diversity of animals and plants that live in vibrant ecosystems. A healthy forest environment is necessary in order for the trees that provide the natural habitat for wildlife to be productive. Many forests control water flow and reduce soil erosion, providing an ecological equilibrium to sustain the forest life. Concern exists that if the present potential for logging activities is realized, Canadian forests may not be sustainable for the future. For example, approximately 97% of the available timberland of the boreal forest is licensed for logging, the vast majority of which is done through clear-cutting. Extensive clear-cutting is a concern to environmentalists and conservationists as affected areas experience soil erosion and a loss of animal species because of the desert-like landscape that results. However, clear-cutting is preferred by the majority of logging operations across Canada for safety reasons for loggers and because of lower costs. Other forest harvesting methods such as strip logging, shelterwood cutting, and selection cutting have been used in some places.

As a nation, Canadians depend on forests to provide for daily needs, such as housing. Forestry contributes to the national economy and many communities in Canada are dependent upon forestry as a resource-based industry. Protecting forests is a major priority for Canadians, and environmental initiatives such as forest management plans are mandatory in Ontario. These plans require that logging companies present long-term goals for logging areas that incorporate careful plans to protect wildlife and maintain sustainable forests.

2.1.2   describe how natural systems influence cultural and economic activities

HOW NATURAL SYSTEMS INFLUENCE CULTURAL AND ECONOMIC ACTIVITIES

Natural systems such as climate, soil, natural vegetation, wildlife, and landforms influence the cultural and economic activities in Canada in a variety of ways. For example, many employment opportunities, recreational activities, and transportation systems are dependent upon the natural systems that exist throughout Canada's unique ecozones. The geographic environment influences daily interactions. In fact, many economic activities and environmental initiatives reflect a need to for clean air, fresh water, and food, all of which can be derived from natural systems.

Biomes—The sustainability of forests is important because plants and trees produce oxygen and purify the air that is needed for survival. Good soil is crucial to growing enough food to adequately feed the population base. Additionally, there are many animal species, such as bees, butterflies, and birds, that play a role in pollinating at least one third of the foods that are eaten.

Water—Fresh water, either that which flows underground or on land, is required for industrial activity, recreation, agriculture, and daily human requirements. About 25 percent of Canadians are dependent on drilled groundwater for agricultural, industrial, or household uses. Additionally, waterways make up many important transportation systems.

Landforms—Lands often contain rich deposits of valuable minerals that are sources of energy and can drive the economy of resource-based communities. Some landforms are more suitable than others to human interactions. For example, mountains can, at times, pose a barrier to settlement, road building, and many economic activities. Some mountainous areas, however, are more accessible and can support economic activities and provide exceptional natural settings for cultural activities, tourism, and recreation. A significant amount of many people's time is spent taking part in nature-related activities such as skiing, camping, and hiking.

Climate—Many daily cultural and economic activities, as well as the functioning of transportation systems, are dependent upon local and regional weather conditions. The success of agriculture across the country is dependent upon suitable seasonal weather. Climate is a key factor in determining the type of vegetation that the ecosystems within any given area will produce. Climate is also an important factor that influences the working conditions of many resource-based industries in the country. People routinely check weather forecasts to learn if they need to adjust their plans to suit the weather. When people plan holidays, the weather of their destinations is inevitably considered. Heavy snowfall, sleet, and freezing rain can severely impact human activities by causing congestion and delays in transportation systems. Anticipating seasonal weather can help people to plan and modify their activities throughout the year. There is very little that can help people to plan for extreme weather, such as hurricanes and tornados, which can occur very quickly and heavily impact all of the cultural and economic activities within affected areas.

Natural systems affect cultural and economic activities continually as all environmental interactions are in some way connected to the dynamic and interacting natural systems that exist.

2.1.3 describe the regional distribution of Canada's energy sources and the relative importance of each source

REGIONAL DISTRIBUTION AND IMPORTANCE OF CANADA'S ENERGY SOURCES

Canada has an abundant supply of energy resources. As a result of world demand, Canada has become a major exporter of energy resources. At home, Canadians use large amounts of energy. This is partially a result of the geographic factors that shape the country, such as size, which necessitates large amounts of energy for the transportation of people and goods. Some energy resources are derived from minerals, such as oil and natural gas, which are known as fossil fuels. Great amounts of energy are also produced through hydroelectricity.

Canada's main energy sources are not evenly distributed across the country. For example, coal comes mainly from southern and central Alberta. Though coal is presently not as popular a fuel choice in Canada as it once was, it is used in the Great Lakes steel and automotive industries and is in demand by a number of foreign countries. Canada's fuel minerals such as oil and natural gas are primarily located in the interior plains region of the country. Some deposits are also located in the Arctic, and oil has been located and sourced from the continental shelves beneath the sea floor that lie in ocean waters off the coast of Eastern Canada. Canada's modern industries and economic activities are very dependent on the energy that is derived from oil. For example, oil is required to produce gasoline and plastics.

As a result of Canada's large amounts of running water, more hydroelectric power is produced in Canada than in any other country in the world. Hydroelectricity is used as an energy source for many industries and modern conveniences, including most household appliances. There are a number of benefits associated with the use of hydroelectricity, including that it is inexpensive to produce and does not pollute the environment. However, environmental concern exists over ecological damage that occurs when dams are built to keep water flowing year round. Hydro projects are also expensive to start. A large number of Canada's major hydroelectric generation stations are concentrated in British Columbia, Ontario, and Quebec, though a number of predominantly smaller stations do exist throughout Canada's interior.

In Canada, alternative energy sources, such as biomass, wind, and solar technology, are also being pursued in order to provide alternative energy solutions and promote the sustainability of communities. For example, there are more than 80 wind farms presently in operation in Canada, with Canada's wind resource distributed throughout rural areas of the country. Currently, wind farms in Canada have a capacity to produce approximately one percent of Canada's electricity demand with greater capacity projected for the future as more wind farms are under construction.

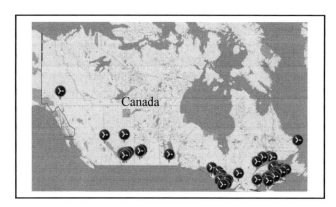

2.1.4   identify the role of government in managing resources and protecting the environment

THE ROLE OF GOVERNMENT IN MANAGING RESOURCES AND PROTECTING THE ENVIRONMENT

The government plays a significant role in managing Canada's natural resources and protecting the environment. In fact, the Canadian provinces and territories have control over the majority of natural resources within the country. Natural Resources Canada works in partnership with all levels of government, research institutes, international organizations, and universities to promote the **responsible use and sustainable development** of Canada's natural resources for future generations.

A number of government initiatives have been taken in order to protect the natural systems within the Canadian environment. The creation and maintenance of national, provincial, and territorial parks systems has sought to protect and preserve many ecological areas within Canada. Presently, Canada also protects parts of ecosystems by building ecological and conservation areas and having particular areas set aside as World Heritage sites.

A recent example of a political endeavor that was taken to protect Canada's natural resources was a $2 billion ecoENERGY initiative. This government initiative seeks to promote the environmentally smart use of energy, increased use of clean energy sources such as biofuels, and modifications to traditional energy sources already in use in Canada in order to ensure their cleaner use. Planned regulations developed by Environment Canada seek a future five percent renewable content of gasoline and a two percent renewable content in heating oil and diesel. It is estimated that the reduction of greenhouse gas emissions by these measures (approximately four megatons) will equal taking almost one million vehicles out of use.

Government at all levels in Canada has taken steps to safeguard natural resources and potential ecological damage to natural systems. In Ontario, the provincial government stipulated that by 2010, 10 percent of the province's power must come from renewable sources.

2.1.5   explain the ways in which the traditional ecological knowledge of Aboriginal People, including their concepts of place, wilderness, and boundaries, influences how they interact with their environment

HOW TRADITIONAL ECOLOGICAL KNOWLEDGE OF ABORIGINAL PEOPLES INFLUENCES THEIR INTERACTIONS WITH THE ENVIRONMENT

In the past, geographers, scientists, and planners contributed to the knowledge of Canada's natural regions through information gathered about the natural environment. In recent years, geographical study has focused on better understanding how the different parts of the environment fit together into interacting systems, referred to as **systems thinking**. The interrelationships between humans and their surrounding environment form the basis of systems thinking. When the connections between the different interacting parts of a system in nature are studied, how people and their environment interact and how a sustainable resource system can be promoted are better understood.

Aboriginal Peoples in Canada have a close association with nature and their land. They have long thought about nature through a systems approach, and this type of knowledge use is referred to as **traditional ecological knowledge**, or **TEK**. Great respect is held for Aboriginal Peoples' use of TEK's unique and valuable wisdom about natural systems and the ways in which they interact.

TEK developed over centuries as Aboriginal Peoples interacted in harmony with their environment and held great respect for the natural systems that surrounded them. They developed unique concepts of place and wilderness through a close understanding of the ecology of their lands. The survival of Aboriginal Peoples was dependent on their understanding of the natural cycles within their environment, such as the seasonal migration of animals upon which they depended. Natural systems provided the plant and animal resources upon which Aboriginal Peoples depended for their food and shelter and that influenced their cultural and economic activities. The natural resources that Aboriginal groups derived from their environment often shaped the trading patterns and transportation routes that Aboriginal Peoples used.

Aboriginal Peoples' valuable and unique TEK has gained importance as environmental concerns about the impact of global warming in the Arctic have become a major issue. Aboriginal People's in-depth understanding of the northern ecosystems, including knowledge about animal behaviour, currents, wind, and sea ice will contribute greatly to the understanding of how the northern ecosystems and wildlife habitats have been affected by development and global warming and what can be done to form solutions to help these ecologically impacted natural systems.

2.2.1   assess the value of Canada's key natural resources

ASSESSING THE VALUE OF CANADA'S KEY NATURAL RESOURCES

Canada's natural resources are of exceedingly great ecological, social, cultural, and economic value. Many components of people's lifestyles, including jobs, recreation, and health, are very connected to the natural resources within Canada's natural systems. For example, Canada's forest resources produce life-sustaining oxygen. People receive ecological, aesthetic, and economic benefit directly and indirectly from natural resources. More than one million Canadians work in resource-related industries and in the export of raw materials to other markets.

Water systems—Canada has a large supply of natural freshwater resources, but more than half of that water flows through rivers to the Arctic and is inaccessible to many parts of the country. Canada's water systems are valuable and reliable resources necessary for the viability of many human activities, such as agriculture, fishing, manufacturing, industry, household and recreational use, and thermal and hydroelectric power generation. Canada has four larger water drainage basins: those of the Arctic Ocean, Pacific Ocean, Hudson Bay, and Atlantic Ocean, with a fifth drainage basin located in small sections of Alberta and Saskatchewan that include south-flowing waterways that are part of the Gulf of Mexico drainage basin. Canada's water resources are valuable and necessary to all aspects of human and economic activity in the country.

Fisheries—The coastal waters of Atlantic Canada were historically among the richest fish harvesting areas in the world. A decline in fish numbers has caused hardship for many people who for generations have depended upon fisheries, such as commercial fishing operations, as a valuable natural resource. Fishing in Canada is very important to the lives of many people in many coastal areas, both culturally and economically. As a result of declining numbers of some fish, such as salmon and cod, some of those who work within this resource-based industry have changed to other fish species to harvest, such as shellfish, or taken other types of work. In response to the depletion of fish, aquaculture, or fish farming, has grown rapidly as an industry on the east and west coasts and in inland areas.

Agricultural lands—These lands, which are an important natural resource, are spread intermittently across Canada, predominantly in southern areas of Eastern Canada and central southern areas of the western interior of the country. More than 10 percent of the country's population is employed in agriculture. Although Canada has an abundant supply of fresh food, agricultural lands are limited, with only seven percent of Canada's lands being arable (capable of growing crops). Decisions on how to use agricultural lands are based on natural factors, such as climate, soils, and landforms, and human factors, such as consumer demands, the need for nearby transportation and markets, and competition. Technological advances that have been applied to agricultural lands have produced higher crop yields, but have at times increased environmental and health concerns. Today, many farms are very large and require fewer people to operate. Many urban centres have spread into prime agricultural lands, and politicians, planners, and environmentalists are determining ways to ensure the use of these valuable lands for sustainable agriculture.

Forested lands—Half of Canada's total land area is forest, with the majority containing trees suitable for the production of materials and products. Forested lands cover large parts of a number of Canada's ecozones. For example, more than 90 percent of the Atlantic Maritime ecozone is covered in forest. Canada's forested lands are of tremendous value to Canadians, and productivity and sustainability of these forests depend upon maintaining healthy forest ecosystems. Forests contain dynamic and interacting ecosystems of activity and life, containing numerous animal and plant species that live throughout the forest's natural habitats. As well, within these ecosystems, constant life cycles of trees and plant organisms carefully interact with other natural systems to reduce soil erosion, control water flow, and filter air, producing oxygen and storing carbon. With such complex dynamics at play, the sustainability of forests is of great importance and has become an environmental concern to many people.

Rainforests—Many coastal areas of British Columbia consist of spectacular rainforests. These beautiful areas are host to a number of unique ecosystems of plants and animals. The rainforests are composed of a canopy of giant coniferous trees, such as cedar, hemlock, and spruce, with a dense layer of bushes and shrubs below. The rainforest floor and lower trunks of trees are covered with an assortment of wet mosses and ferns, with pools of rainwater interspersed. The potential for medicines derived from rainforest plants is exceptional, and rainforests are a valuable ecological and cultural natural resource.

Minerals—Mining occurs when a substantial amount of minerals exist in a given space, thus making a mining operation economically feasible. For example, metallic minerals such as nickel and copper are mined from deposits found within igneous rocks located in the Canadian Shield. Mineral production, which occurs in all provinces and territories, supplies necessary raw materials that are required for Canada's industries. Many resource-based communities have been built to provide services and support mining operations. Mineral production plays a strong role in Canada's economy because of demand within the nation and overseas. Canada is one of the largest exporters worldwide of minerals and mineral-based products.

Fuel minerals—Coal, natural gas, and oil are primarily produced in the western interior of Canada, but oil and gas fields also exist in areas of offshore Atlantic Canada and the Arctic. Oil and natural gas are extracted from between rock layers. Canada's industrial and economic activities are very dependent on oil energy. For example, oil is required to produce gasoline and tar. Many of Canada's fossil fuels are exported to other countries to meet their energy needs.

2.2.2   assess the feasibility of using selected renewable and alternative energy sources (e.g., solar, wind, tidal, hydrogen fuel cell) to implement conservation strategies

ASSESSING THE FEASIBILITY OF USING SELECTED RENEWABLE AND ALTERNATIVE ENERGY SOURCES

Canada's natural resources are of exceptional value to the Canadian quality of life. In order to promote the sustainability of Canada's energy sources within the environment, technologies and strategies have been used to further develop and use renewable and alternate energy sources. Harnessing energy sources that serve to slow global warming and protect Canada's ecozones while complementing the availability of energy that is needed for the economy influences a sustainable resource system for the future.

Biofuels—The Canadian government is committed to expanding the development, production, and use of cleaner and renewable fuel types (biofuels) and the modification of traditional fuel sources through the addition of biofuel content to those sources. Ethanol and biodiesel, which are made from different forms of plant matter, are biofuels. Efforts to use biofuels have been taken in order to decrease greenhouse gas emissions from automobile fuel use. A number of ethanol plants have been built in Ontario. Because corn has risen in cost as a result of its demand in producing ethanol, some farmers who rely on corn to feed livestock are concerned about the extra costs to maintain their farms and the costs to consumers for meat products.

Solar—This type of power derives energy directly from the sun. **Passive solar power**, which has existed for thousands of years, occurs when the sun enters through windows and heat is absorbed into walls, floors, and furniture that radiate back heat energy. Large, south-facing double-paned windows in major buildings allow natural winter heating. Recently, **active solar power** has shown great future promise through the usage of solar panels to heat buildings. Present forms of solar power are expensive. Photovoltaic cells also show promise as devices used to convert sunlight to electricity, but efficiency and cost are being pursued to make them a more economic means to serve energy needs.

Wind—Wind energy has been used for hundreds of years and many wind farms have been created in recent years in Canada to meet energy demands and environmental concern of the environment. Wind turbines are power energy producers that require no fuel. One issue that has been considered is finding locations to build wind farms where the winds are not too strong to damage the turbine parts. As wind farms can be built in locations close to economic markets, they are a feasible source of energy that show much promise. Wind farms in Canada currently have a capacity to produce approximately one percent of Canada's electricity demands, with greater capacity projected for the future.

Tidal—Tidal energy also offers a clean energy solution, but unique geographic circumstances of water flow and tide strength influence where such projects can be built. A tidal energy project exists at Annapolis Royal, Nova Scotia, where a dam was built across the Annapolis River in order to harness tidal energy from the strong tides in the Bay of Fundy. Water gates open when the tide flows up the river and water enters a nearby lagoon. At low tide, the gates open and the outpouring water serves to turn a large turbine, thus generating hydroelectricity.

Hydrogen fuel cell—No waste is produced by hydrogen fuel cells, which do not require recharging. These fuel cells produce energy by combining a hydrogen fuel source with oxygen. Vehicles using hydrogen fuel cells run on electric motors and only emit water and water vapour. A number of buses in Canadian cities run on hydrogen fuel cells.

2.2.3   evaluate differing viewpoints on the benefits and disadvantages of selected resource megaprojects

EVALUATING DIFFERING VIEWPOINTS ON THE BENEFITS AND DISADVANTAGES OF SELECTED RESOURCE MEGAPROJECTS

In an attempt to maximize the potential resource base in a given area, some resource projects have developed and constructed very large megaprojects. Differing views exist on the benefits and disadvantages of a number of projects of this type.

James Bay hydro complex—Hydro projects are extremely large and expensive structures to build. The first stage of the James Bay hydro complex, which occurred in the early 1970s, cost $21 billion in start-up costs. The project involved the diversion of several rivers that had naturally flowed into James Bay. These rivers were diverted into a huge man-made lake situated behind several dams. The energy that resulted from the project was used in Quebec and in the United States, which purchased part of the energy produced. The project attracted great environmental concern as much of the local and interconnected ecosystems were affected by changes to wildlife habitats. For example, as a result of the project, the Caniapiscau River, which had previously been a narrow waterway, became a 10-kilometre-wide lake. An ecological disaster occurred in 1984 when 10 000 caribou that were following their yearly migration were not able to swim the distance across what had been the Caniapiscau River and drowned. Environmental effects such as these have also affected Aboriginal Peoples who lived nearby and depended upon the caribou for their food. During the early 1990s, stage two of the project met with opposition from many people and eventually it was cancelled even though $13 billion had already been spent.

Hibernia offshore oil field—The Hibernia offshore oil field is located in an ocean area off the eastern coast of Newfoundland and is jointly owned by a number of oil field companies. The completed 224-metre high drilling platform was towed and positioned to the sea floor by a number of platforms in 1997. Unique to offshore drilling, oil platforms are constructed to lie on the ocean floor as the drilling takes place underwater. Environmental concern exists because of the chance of an oil spill into ocean waters as the ecological ramifications would be immense.

Athabasca oil sands—Great amounts of oil are located in the sand and shale of northern Alberta's Athabasca oil sands, or tar sands. The oil is present in a thick sand and oil mixture. The oil sands area is immense in size and the drilling of these sands is of great economic value because of a very large US market. The amount of water necessary from the Athabasca River to wash the oil from the sand before it can travel by pipeline to southern refineries is huge and increasing in demand. As a result, the volume of water that flows in the Athabasca River has decreased by about 30 percent over the last 30 years. To add to this ecological concern, plans are underway to build a 3 000 square foot open-pit mine that will require the use of more water for its operations. Ecological concern exists because the waters of the Athabasca River are not sustainable to these economic demands. The river water has become polluted, which has damaged the fragile ecosystem to the point where water from the Athabasca River is no longer fit to drink and the fish are no longer suitable to eat. Waterfowl are often unable to fly because of the oil that gets stuck in their feathers and many have been poisoned by the oil. Fish have also been affected by the oil, which can stick to their gills. The economy of the area is thriving with many jobs and economic profitability; however, environmental concern exists regarding the sustainability of the natural systems.

2.2.4   assess how the effects of urban growth alter the natural environment

THE AFFECTS OF URBAN GROWTH ON THE NATURAL ENVIRONMENT

Urban growth can greatly impact the landscape of natural environments. Some areas of prime farmland have been encroached upon by expanding urban development, or urban sprawl. The landscape of the Great Lakes and St. Lawrence River basin has been changed over the last century because of urbanization. Over the last hundred years, populations have steadily shifted from rural to urban centres. In Quebec, population grew primarily along the banks of the St. Lawrence River where more than 80 percent of the province's population now lives. In Ontario, close to 90 percent of the province's population lives around the Great Lakes (the Golden Horseshoe region). Development in areas of potential farmland has occurred in these regions, which is where some of Canada's richest farmland is located. Rising costs of land due to proximity to urban centres have made some of this land unattainable to farmers. Consequently, the lands have gone toward development activities. As only approximately seven percent of Canada's land area is arable (capable of growing crops), this loss of farmland is of great concern to future food productivity. Additionally, the natural wildlife habitat of local ecosystems is impacted, altered, or removed as a result of urban growth. The balance and interconnection of these natural systems sustain much wildlife habitat. Thus, urban growth can lead to the endangerment and loss of species.

Marshes are areas of wetland characterized by cattails and grasses. Marshes are nurseries that are home to many species of insects, fish, reptiles, plants, and other living organisms. Marshes provide valuable food access and habitat for waterfowl such as herons, swans, and ducks. Some birds and wildlife face possible extinction as urban development has led to the draining of areas of natural marshland in order to provide lands for urban growth. In some cases, the draining of marshes has completely eliminated some species of wildlife. The Great Blue Heron is an example of a bird whose existence is threatened by human activities. In southern Ontario, areas of marsh habitat are in shorter supply than in previous years. This presents an ecological challenge as these open water areas of habitat are vital to both local species and migratory wildlife. In the Mixedwood Plains ecozone, more than 90 percent of wetland areas have experienced drainage to accommodate agriculture or urban development.

Measures have been taken to try and protect areas of fertile soil and marshland and to contain urban sprawl. In Ontario, the government has devised a plan to control urban sprawl in the Golden Horseshoe area. In 2005, the government mandated that areas of green space, called greenbelts, be established around cities in order to better preserve and conserve bordering areas of natural lands. Additionally, there are plans to control urban sprawl and protect farmland that include determining that 40 percent of new growth must take place in already built-up areas by 2015 and urban areas must become more compact communities that rely more on public transit. These measures also strive to protect 720 000 hectares of green space lands that are located between Peterborough and Niagara.

Environmental awareness to other areas facing loss of wildlife habitat and arable lands continues to influence discussion and measures of trying to conserve the biodiversity of these valuable ecological regions.

2.2.5   present findings from research on ways of improving the balance between human and natural systems

RESEARCHING AND PRESENTING WAYS TO IMPROVE THE BALANCE BETWEEN HUMAN AND NATURAL SYSTEMS

Research provides ideas and avenues that can lead to improving the balance between human and natural systems within the environment. This research involves the study of activities that protect, restore, and preserve the environment, thus improving the sustainability of natural systems and ensuring the quality of life of Canadians and future generations. Areas of research can involve river clean-ups, ecological restoration of woodlots or schoolyards, initiatives to conserve energy supplies, natural resource sustainability, or industrial initiatives to reduce emissions. There are many ways of improving the balance between human and natural systems.

While conducting research, questions provide a framework for inquiry from which you can gather, analyze, evaluate, and present your findings. For example, what actions have been taken to improve the balance between human and natural systems in the environment? Why were these actions necessary? How were these actions beneficial to the environment? Could these actions be repeated or modified and then applied to other similar situations in other places to gain even greater environmental benefit? These and other questions can guide you in gaining information that you can present about ways to improve the balance between Earth's human and natural systems.

2.3.1   analyse and evaluate the success, in environmental and economic terms, of local waste management methods

ANALYZING AND EVALUATING THE SUCCESS OF LOCAL WASTE MANAGEMENT METHODS

Waste is created when human systems interact with the environment. Earth's natural features have changed over time as a result. For example, emissions have been released into the atmosphere, a number of waterways have been polluted, and some farming and logging practices can erode the soil. Some human activities such as recycling and crop rotation help Earth's natural environment by reducing waste and protecting the environment. Natural cycles within the environment include processes that naturally decompose and recycle all waste materials within forests and throughout natural settings. As human systems interact with Earth's natural systems, the challenge becomes finding ways to effectively recycle and manage the disposal of waste that is created by these interactions and decrease the use of harmful wastes that are toxic to people and the environment.

The health of people and the health of the environment are closely linked. What affects soils and water systems also affects the people who drink the water and work on or interact with the land. Waste that is managed effectively will have long-lasting positive effects on local wildlife habitats and people. It will also lead to more productive methods of conducting economic activities such as manufacturing and providing services that support communities.

Part of your initial research may involve collecting information about local waste management methods and categorizing this information in a visual organizer. Some questions to guide your research may be similar to the following:

• What kinds of recycling and composting activities exist in your community?

• What other types of waste management exist in your community?

• Are these forms of waste management effective? Why or why not?

- What are common pollutants in your community and how do they affect the ecosystems?

- What are ways to reduce or limit the affect of these pollutants?

- Can these pollutants be replaced?

- Where is local waste disposed of or recycled?

- Is this ecologically effective and/or economically effective?

Analyzing and evaluating your local waste management methods will involve topics such as the proven effectiveness, economic viability, and short- and long-term effects on people and the environment.

The process of analyzing and evaluating the success of waste management methods in your community will actively involve you in making decisions and forming conclusions about effective ways to manage waste and promote sustainability of Earth's ecosystems. Through this process, you may also think of and create other solutions to waste management that can be implemented in either your local community or your school community.

2.3.2 *evaluate solutions to environmental problems proposed by various groups (e.g., by government, industry, environmentalists, community members) and make recommendations for sustainable resource use*

EVALUATING SOLUTIONS TO ENVIRONMENTAL PROBLEMS PROPOSED BY VARIOUS GROUPS AND MAKING RECOMMENDATIONS FOR SUSTAINABLE RESOURCE USE

Discussion by various groups has generated solutions to ecological problems within the environment. Proposed ideas have included dialogue about smarter and greener solutions and ensuring sustainability of the natural resources within Canada's environment, such as sustainable agriculture, sustainable forestry, and sustainable economic development. These ideas have prompted awareness by many Canadians that changes need to be made that can promote the protection and preservation of the natural environment.

Evaluating these proposed solutions leads to recommendations for long-lasting sustainable resource use. Acting upon such suggestions can foster the protection of Canada's natural resources so that they can be enjoyed and used by future generations of Canadians and ecozones can be thriving environments of plant and wildlife habitat, free from the threat of depletion and extinction.

Your research should involve developing a criterion on which to decide, for each proposed solution, its effectiveness as a solution to a particular environmental problem. Factors to consider include each solution's intended outcomes, cost (environmental and economic), benefits to human and natural systems, and possible unintended outcomes.

Analyze the proposed solutions to environmental problems and conclude, with gathered information and reasoning, those recommendations that you feel show great potential and would be of ecological value to pursue. Try to take these ideas and view these possibilities in new ways, or make some changes that you think may improve their effectiveness as solutions. Creating, or synthesizing, new ideas toward environmental problems can lead to the development of even stronger solutions. You have already learned about proposed solutions to environmental problems. Now, your role as an effective environmental problem-solver is to evaluate the proposed solutions to environmental problems and recommend those and others that will best promote sustainable natural and economic systems of today for future generations.

2.3.3   recommend ways in which individuals can contribute to the quality of life in their home, local ecozone, province, nation, and the world

QUALITY OF LIFE

Individuals of all ages can contribute to the quality of life in their home, local ecozone, province, nation, and the world. The world and the human and natural systems that interact within it are connected in very unique ways. Finding ways to promote the quality of life for people and the balance within their human and natural systems will serve to promote the sustainability of natural resources and the protection of biodiversity within ecosystems. This, in turn, can reduce the ecological footprint and ensure the quality of life for future generations and the sustainability of the natural environment.

How can individuals contribute to Canada's quality of life? List all of the suggestions that come to mind, such as the use of alternate forms of energy (a number of student classes have built solar ovens and tested them), recycling, schoolyard restoration, composting, and planting gardens. List your suggestions in a visual organizer such as a web or chart and then expand through inquiry upon these suggestions. Little steps can lead to long-lasting and effective changes that can positively impact and improve the quality of life in human and natural systems.

AN EXAMPLE OF ACTION TAKEN TO PROMOTE ENVIRONMENTAL SUSTAINABILITY AND THE QUALITY OF LIFE—AN INITIATIVE BY STUDENTS AND SCIENCE TEACHERS AT COCHRANE HIGH SCHOOL, COCHRANE, ALBERTA.

At Cochrane High School, plans were started in 2000 for a sustainable energy initiative involving solar power that could promote sustainability of the environment and improve quality of life of the environment. Through the efforts of fifteen students on the school's Sustainable Development Committee and their science teachers, $50 000 was raised through fundraising, donations, and grants that enabled their project to be realized. In 2004, 30 solar panels were installed on the roof of the school and tied to the building's power grid, along with a 400-watt wind turbine. This initiative generates approximately one percent of the school's power needs and was one of the first initiatives of this type for any school in Canada, garnering the attention of Canadian environmentalist David Suzuki, as well as national recognition. Having completed the project, one Grade 12 student noted, "All our hard work has paid off, and we hope people will be able to follow in our footsteps in the near future."

Source: quote from The Cochrane Times, "CHS Goes Green – Emerald Green" by Catherine Oshanek, June 22, 2005

PRACTICE QUESTIONS—HUMAN-ENVIRONMENT INTERACTIONS

1. Urban sprawl would most likely have a negative impact on all of the following **except**
   A. potential agriculture
   B. wildlife habitats
   C. marshes
   D. industry

2. Which of the following activities would be least affected by climate conditions in Canada?
   A. Fishing
   B. Farming
   C. Recreation
   D. Manufacturing

3. The **main** reason that coal is not used as often in Canada as it once was is that it
   A. is expensive to produce
   B. is preferred by Canada's foreign markets
   C. produces large amounts of greenhouse gas emissions
   D. has been mined in Canada nearly to the point of depletion

4. The Canadian government implemented the ecoENERGY initiative in order to promote all of the following actions **except**
   A. modifying fossil fuel energy sources in use
   B. increasing the use of clean energy sources
   C. using environmentally smarter energy sources
   D. increasing the production of traditional energy sources

Use the following information to answer the next question.

Traditional ecological knowledge of Aboriginal Peoples is used to help with understanding how natural systems within the environment have been impacted by global warming that occurs as a result of economic activities.

5. Which of the following parts of the Arctic environment has **most likely** been least impacted by climate change?
   A. Ice
   B. Wildlife
   C. Vegetation
   D. Marine areas

6. The **main** reason that Canada's agricultural lands are often considered a renewable resource is that

    A. agricultural lands in a particular area primarily receive similar weather every year

    B. crops like wheat and corn are hardy and can continue to grow year after year

    C. properly cared for soils can sustain crop growth for many years

    D. agricultural lands often contain oil and natural gas deposits

7. The government requires that which of the following renewable or alternate energy sources be added to some traditional fuels in order to make emissions cleaner?

    A. Biofuels

    B. Wind power

    C. Hydroelectricity

    D. Hydrogen fuel cells

8. The **greatest** benefits of the Athabasca oil sands project are

    A. environmental

    B. economic

    C. cultural

    D. health

9. Which of the following activities would **best** improve the balance between human and natural systems?

    A. People white-water rafting down a river

    B. Restoring a schoolyard to its natural state

    C. Using the fur from animals to make fashion boots

    D. Adding attractive tropical flower beds to golf courses

10. Which of the following activities would **not** contribute to the quality of life in a person's home and community?

    A. Planting a vegetable garden

    B. Pouring out old paint down the drain

    C. Helping a friend's family build a shelterbelt around their farm

    D. Throwing organic material from meals into an outside compost

ANSWERS AND SOLUTIONS—PRACTICE QUESTIONS

1. D	3. C	5. C	7. A	9. B
2. D	4. D	6. C	8. B	10. B

1. D

Factories that exist on lands that spread out from urban centres are an example of urban sprawl. Valuable ecological lands are often damaged or destroyed when industries are built in areas that spread out from cities.

Agricultural lands are often threatened or eliminated by urban sprawl. Wildlife habitats and marshes, which contain fragile ecosystems, are also threatened and destroyed by urban sprawl.

2. D

Manufacturing mainly takes place indoors and is not as dependent upon climatic factors as the other given alternatives. Fishing is dependent at times upon seasonal weather. Farming is dependent upon climatic factors such as the length of growing seasons and the amount of precipitation that an area receives.

The viability of many recreational activities is dependent upon the climate. Skiing takes place mainly during colder snowy months, and outdoor golf takes place during warmer months.

3. C

Although coal is still used in Great Lakes industries, it is not as popular a choice as it once was because of the high amounts of greenhouse gas emissions that it produces. Coal is not overly expensive to produce. While coal is in high demand by a number of Canada's foreign markets, this is not a reason it is not as popular in Canada as an energy source as it once was. There is an ample supply of coal in southern Alberta.

4. D

Increasing the production of traditional energy sources is not a factor that the ecoENERGY initiative promotes. The government initiative seeks to modify traditional energy sources (fossil fuels) already in use in Canada so as to ensure their cleaner use. Increasing the use of clean energy sources and using environmentally smarter energy sources are intentions of the ecoENERGY initiative.

5. C

Since not a lot of vegetation can grow in Arctic areas, vegetation is not as heavily impacted by climate change as the other given alternatives. The melting of sea ice is of great environmental concern because it impacts ocean temperatures, which in turn impact world climates. Wildlife is also impacted by climate change. For example, melting ice causes the polar bears' hunting season to be shorter and therefore they cannot acquire the amount of food that they need to survive, and Aboriginal Peoples' who depend on wildlife for sustenance must find other forms of food. Marine areas are deeply affected by climate change as the natural balance of life in these ecological areas is disrupted.

6. C

Canada's agricultural lands are often considered to be renewable because soils that are properly cared for can often grow crops year after year. The fact that agricultural lands in a particular area receive similar weather every year and that some crops may be more resistant to disease are not reasons that these lands are considered renewable. The majority of Canada's agricultural lands do not contain oil or natural gas deposits.

7. A

The government requires that biofuels be added to traditional fuels in order to decrease emissions. Wind power, hydroelectricity, and hydrogen fuel cells are not added to traditional fuels to decrease emissions.

8. B

The oil sands project has been extremely profitable to oil companies and Aboriginal Peoples living in the area. Most notably, unemployment is practically non-existent. The greatest benefit for Aboriginal Peoples and others living and working on these lands has been economic, although some of the funds generated from the economic development of the oil sands may have been directed toward cultural activities or facilities.

There have been many environmental disadvantages to the oil sands project, such as pollution of the Athabasca River and damages to the health of birds, fish, and possibly people. Health benefits from the oil sands project are extremely unlikely. The Athabasca River has been deemed too polluted to fish in and wildlife has been impacted by the oil sands activity.

9. B

Restoring a schoolyard to its natural state would benefit the natural resources, such as soils, plants, and trees, of the original environment and could lead to greater preservation and conservation of those resources for the future.

White-water rafting and using animal fur to make fashion boots would not serve to improve the balance between human and natural systems. Building golf courses necessitates stripping the land of its original plant and wildlife habitat. Since the tropical flower beds that are planted are not naturally found in the local ecosystem, they may be aesthetically beautiful, but they would certainly not improve the balance between human and natural systems in the ecosystem.

10. B

Pouring out old paint down the drain contaminates the water supply. Paint should be disposed of at an ecological depot created for such purposes.

Planting a vegetable garden provides people with fresh foods and uses the soils in an ecologically friendly way. A shelterbelt built around a farm serves to protect crops from winds and the soil from erosion. These natural resources are thus protected. Composting recycles unused foods into useful organic waste that can be used in planting. Composting diverts waste from landfills and therefore conserves landfill space.

UNIT TEST—HUMAN-ENVIRONMENT INTERACTIONS

1. Near which of the following economic activities would a resource-based community **most likely** be built?

   A. Lumber sales

   B. Tourist venue

   C. Diamond mine

   D. Food-processing plant

2. Which of the following approaches is the **most effective** way of ensuring that more Canadians take part in recycling?

   A. Distribution of more blue boxes

   B. Offering more jobs in the recycling industry

   C. Providing a wider variety of collection approaches

   D. Passing legislation that makes recycling mandatory

3. Which of the following natural systems would **most likely** present the greatest challenge to road-builders in British Columbia?

   A. Wildlife

   B. Climate

   C. Natural landforms

   D. Natural vegetation

4. Employment within which of the following industries has been **most** negatively impacted in Canada by the over-depletion of natural resources?

   A. Furniture manufacturing

   B. Jewelry making

   C. Farming

   D. Fishing

5. Which of the following energy sources is produced very profitably in provinces across Canada?

   A. Oil

   B. Wind power

   C. Natural gas

   D. Hydroelectricity

6. Which of the following energy sources is located in very close proximity to natural gas?

   A. Oil

   B. Tar

   C. Coal

   D. Water

7. An example of a modification to a traditional energy source that is supported by the Canadian government is

   A. corn added to bio-diesel

   B. ethanol added to gasoline

   C. bio-diesel added to ethanol

   D. tidal vapour added to natural gas

8. The **main** reason the Ontario government requires that 10 percent of future power come from renewable sources is to

   A. find alternative ways to power Ontario's industries

   B. find solutions to Ontario's power shortage

   C. promote a sustainable environment

   D. cut down on pollution

9. Aboriginal Peoples living in the Arctic **most likely** use TEK for all of the following activities except for

   A. cooking a meal

   B. hunting caribou

   C. travelling by boat

   D. designing outdoor clothing

10. The **most likely** reason that Aboriginal Peoples developed traditional ecological knowledge over time was as a response to their

    A. need to survive

    B. respect for nature

    C. desire to be successful traders

    D. need to use the best transportation routes

11. Environmentalists do not care for the clear-cutting logging method for all of the following reasons **except**

    A. all of the trees in a given area are removed

    B. soil erosion occurs in the area following clear-cutting

    C. clear-cutting is a dangerous method of forest harvesting for loggers

    D. there is a loss of biodiversity in the area as animals and tree species can disappear

12. Which of the following types of land use **most likely** damages natural resources the most?

    A. Industrial land use

    B. Institutional land use

    C. Commercial land use

    D. Recreational land use

ANSWERS AND SOLUTIONS—UNIT TEST

1. C	4. D	7. B	10. A
2. C	5. D	8. C	11. C
3. C	6. A	9. A	12. A

1. C

Diamonds are a primary resource derived from the environment in its natural state. Resource-based communities often build up around primary industries in rural areas. Lumber sales and tourist venues are examples of tertiary industries. Food-processing industries are secondary industries.

2. C

Providing a wide variety of collection approaches would give people an opportunity to recycle a greater number of items of varying sizes and uses at a variety of convenient locations. The blue box program was a very successful environmental initiative, but additional needs do exist for the recycling of larger materials and industrial waste, and for greater numbers of people to participate in recycling. The number of jobs that could be created would be small compared with the number of people who should be recycling. It would be difficult to enforce this type of legislation on an individual basis.

3. C

Natural landforms would present the greatest challenge as landforms such as mountains can block routes from being built. Wildlife, climate, and natural vegetation are unlikely to present the greatest challenge to road-builders.

4. D

The fishing industry has been most affected by the depletion of fish species off the coasts of Canada. Many fishermen have had to fish for other species or take other work. As a result, the industry of aquaculture, or fish farming, has grown as an alternate means to harvesting fish. Employment in the furniture manufacturing industry, jewelry making, and agriculture have not been impacted as a result of the over-depletion of natural resources.

5. D

Many hydroelectric stations are built across Canada. Hydroelectricity costs very little to operate and produces no waste. Large amounts of hydroelectricity are sold to the United States. Oil and natural gas are located primarily in the western provinces. Wind farms have emerged in recent years across Canada, but they currently exist on a much smaller scale than sources of hydro energy. As a result, wind farms do not generate the amount of power or economic profitability as hydroelectricity, which is more widespread in availability.

6. A

Natural gas deosits are located above oil and are usually extracted first. Tar is not necessarily located in close proximity to natural gas. Coal is mined and oil and natural gas are drilled. Water is not necessarily located in very close proximity to natural gas.

7. B

Ethanol is a biofuel that is added to gasoline to make up part of its content in order to cut down on emissions. This is an example of a modification to a traditional energy source. Bio-diesel is not a traditional energy source. Neither bio-diesel nor ethanol are traditional energy sources. Natural gas is a traditional energy source, but tidal vapour would not be added to it.

8. C

The government wishes to promote a sustainable environment through the responsible use of natural sources of energy. One of the intended outcomes of this goal is to decrease pollution by using greener energy sources. Promoting a sustainable environment also serves to protect natural resources for future generations. Renewable sources of power are required to provide for all energy needs within the province of Ontario, not just those of industry. This in itself does not explain the reason that the requirement for 10 percent renewable content was made. Ontario does not have a power shortage. Cutting down on pollution is one of the intended outcomes of promoting a sustainable environment.

9. A

While cooking a meal may require an understanding of TEK, it is essential. TEK would, however, be very useful in understanding animal migration patterns and, consequently, in planning hunting trips. TEK would also be very useful when travelling by boat for determining water currents, sea ice, and wind. Additionally, TEK would be very useful in designing outdoor clothing as knowledge of local climate systems would enable clothing to be designed that would best suit the environment.

10. A

Aboriginal Peoples most likely developed TEK as a response to their need to survive, which was dependent on their understanding of natural cycles within their environment, such as animal migration. Aboriginal Peoples have great respect for nature. TEK most likely developed as an understanding of the interconnected systems within nature upon which their survival depended. Aboriginal Peoples undoubtedly desired to be successful traders and needed to use effective transportation routes, but TEK was more likely associated with their need to survive within their natural environment.

11. C

Environmentalists are opposed to clear-cutting for various reasons, but the safety of loggers is not one of them. One of the reasons that clear-cutting is preferred by logging companies is that it can be a safer method of logging for workers. Clear-cutting is also more profitable for logging companies. All of the trees in a given area are removed during clear-cutting. Soil erosion does occur in clear-cut areas because all of the trees have been removed and the soils are no longer set in place by the trees. There is a loss of biodiversity in areas that have had clear-cutting occur as wildlife habitats have been lost or eliminated.

12. A

Industrial land use involves land that is used for factories to manufacture goods, other types of secondary industry, and structures that support those industries, such as warehouses. Industrial land use poses the greatest potential damage to natural resources because this type of land use requires very large areas where the natural habitat is removed, and water, soil, and atmosphere pollution occur as a result.

Commercial land use involves land that is designated for business activities, such as stores on a community's main street or a shopping plaza. Recreational land use involves lands that are used for sporting or social activities, such as playgrounds and golf courses.

Institutional land use involves lands that are used by services provided in a community, such as schools, places of worship, government buildings, and hospitals.

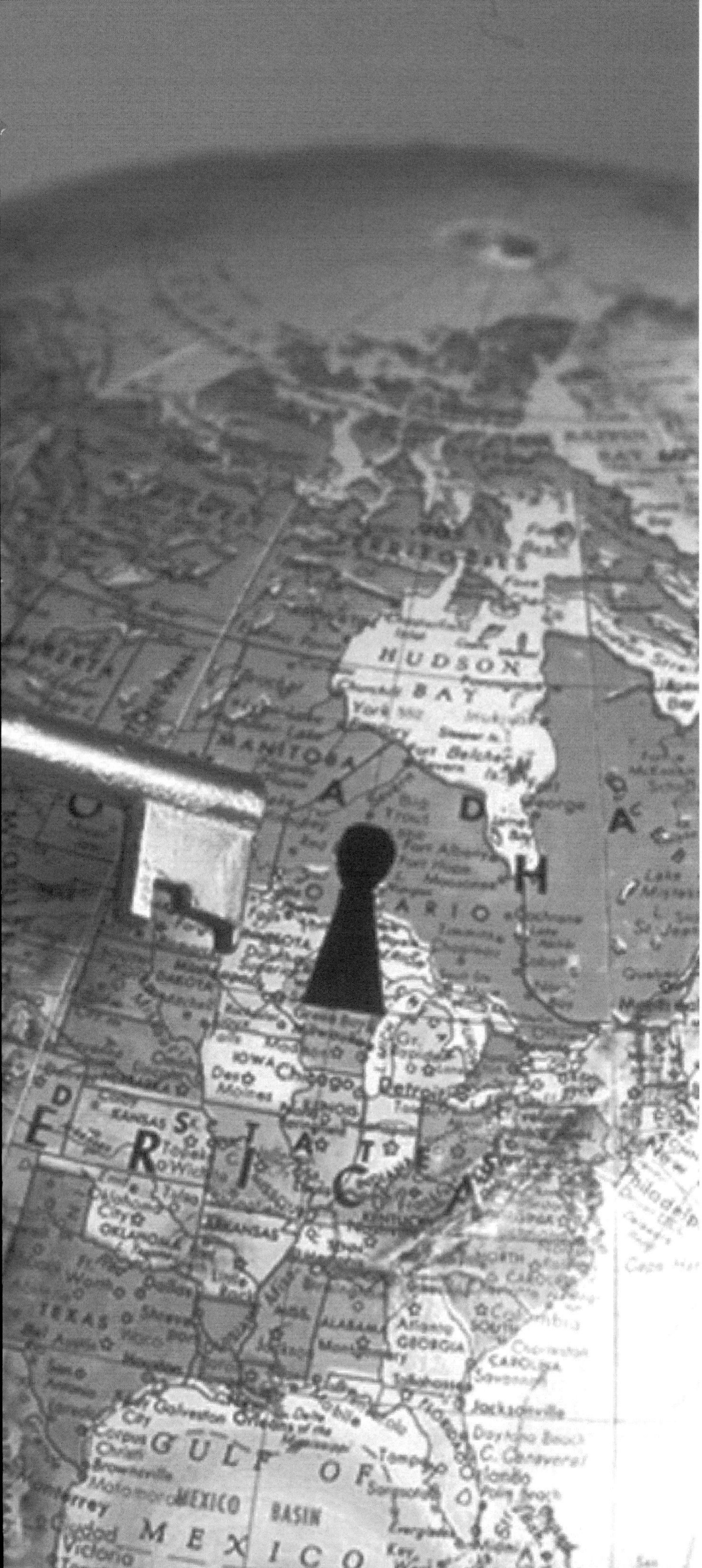

Global Connections

GLOBAL CONNECTIONS

Table of Correlations		
Specific Expectation	**Practice Questions**	**Unit Test Questions**
Students are expected to:		
3.1 *describe how Canada's diverse geography affects its economic, cultural, and environmental links to other countries*		
3.1.1 explain the role of selected international organizations and agreements and why Canada participates in them	1	1, 2
3.1.2 summarize significant contributions Canada makes to the world	2	3, 4
3.1.3 explain how Canada's natural systems form part of global natural systems	3, 4	5, 6
3.2 *analyse connections between Canada and other countries*		
3.2.1 compare Canada's approaches to specific concerns with the approaches of other nations	5	7, 8
3.2.2 evaluate Canada's participation in organizations that deal with global issues	6	9, 10
3.2.3 analyse the global distribution of selected commodities and determine Canada's share of each	7	11, 12
3.2.4 summarize ways in which the economies of Canada and the rest of the world are interdependent	8	13, 14
3.2.5 evaluate the importance of tourism to Canada's economic development	9, 10	15, 16
3.3 *report on global issues that affect Canadians*		
3.3.1 compare, in terms of resource use and consumption, the "ecological footprint" of an average Canadian with that of an average citizen in a developing country	11	17, 18, 20
3.3.2 produce a set of guidelines for developing a solution to a global geographic or environmental issue		19

GLOBAL CONNECTIONS

3.1.1   explain the role of selected international organizations and agreements and why Canada participates in them

CANADIAN PARTICIPATION IN INTERNATIONAL ORGANIZATIONS AND AGREEMENTS

Canada is known globally for its commitment to world peace, cooperation, and the well-being of Earth's natural and human systems. As such, Canada actively assists and protects other countries and communities in the world and promotes economic and environmental activities through its participation in a number of international organizations and agreements.

UNITED NATIONS

Canada is one of nearly 200 countries from around the world that belong to the United Nations (UN). The United Nations is an organization that formed following the Second World War with the desire to create peace, cooperation, and security throughout the countries of the world. Lester B. Pearson was significantly involved in establishing the North Atlantic Treaty Organization (NATO) and the United Nations, which endeavored to ensure security worldwide and to work toward the prevention of other world conflicts. Through his work with the UN, Pearson was also an active participant in creating an international peacekeeping force that continues to maintain global peace today. Canada has made a significant contribution in assisting with a variety of international issues since the formation of the UN in 1945. During that time, Canada has been actively involved in providing service and support to a number of UN initiatives—for example, assisting other countries during times of international need, such as providing assistance following natural disasters, and through an active role in global peacekeeping.

SOMMET DE LA FRANCOPHONIE

Canada hosted the 12th Sommet de la Francophonie in Quebec City during October of 2008. La Francophonie is a global organization that Canada participates in to support the role of its francophone community internationally. The organization includes the involvement of 55 member states and governments and thirteen observer states from five continents that use French as a common language. La Francophonie serves to promote linguistic and cultural diversity, peace, human rights, democracy, education and research, and cooperation toward sustainable development.

WORLD TRADE ORGANIZATION

The World Trade Organization is a group that develops and oversees guidelines concerning international trade. Rules affecting global trade can benefit farmers and businesses. Subsidies are sometimes paid to farmers in wealthier and more industrialized countries, which influences the amount of surplus the farmers can produce. This in turn allows more goods be traded on the world market. As farmers that work in developing countries cannot compete with cheaper imports, their own economies can be impacted. Sometimes farmers are forced to take other work. Some international organizations work to improve trade conditions and help farmers in developing countries market their crops through fair-trade programs.

NORTH AMERICAN FREE TRADE AGREEMENT (NAFTA)

NAFTA is a free trade agreement that was signed by Canada, the United States, and Mexico in 1992, thus forming the world's largest free trade area. The agreement sought to allow and encourage tariff-free trade (in goods and services) between these countries as well as removing a number of fees that had previously existed. This has influenced the creation of some Canadian-based businesses in Mexico. Although NAFTA was created to promote trade and eliminate tariffs (taxes that had been placed on goods entering countries), this did not occur with some goods—for example, softwood lumber, which in 2002 had a tariff of 27% placed on it by the United States in order to protect its forestry industry. This, in turn, had a large economic impact on forestry in Canada, including job loss. In 2006, the dispute ended, and the United States financially compensated Canada for about 80% of the tariffs that had been charged.

KYOTO PROTOCOL

The Kyoto Protocol is designed to limit energy emissions and the production of greenhouse gases that occur in the atmosphere as a result of emissions, much of it produced by industries and automobile use. The Kyoto Protocol, which Canada signed in 2002, seeks to lessen global warming. As a result of this accord, many countries agreed to reduce their emissions by 5% below levels recorded in 1990 by the year 2012. Canada wishes to support the Kyoto Protocol and supports changes that would promote the decrease of greenhouse gases. Measures have been taken by all levels of government in Canada to promote energy conservation and sustainable resource use.

ASIA-PACIFIC ECONOMIC COOPERATION

The Asia-Pacific Economic Cooperation (APEC) is an intergovernmental forum that promotes free trade, cooperation, and economic growth in the Asia-Pacific region. This cooperative group exists on the basis of dialogue and non-binding commitments. At present, APEC has 21 members on four continents that represent a dynamic region of the world. APEC represents an area that accounts for approximately 50% of global population and trade. Canada's role in APEC is very important, as the nation seeks to be actively involved in world trade activities.

3.1.2   summarize significant contributions Canada makes to the world

CANADA'S GLOBAL CONTRIBUTIONS

Canada has made a number of contributions to the world, such as in peacekeeping, telecommunications technology, humanitarian aid, and the arts.

PEACEKEEPING

During the past fifty years, Canada has participated in a number of peacekeeping operations that have evolved over time to address international needs. Canada has steadily been committed in its contribution to United Nations peace missions. The support of Canada toward these peace operations helps to bring stability and aid to a number of situations in a variety of locations. The role of a peacekeeper includes a range of diplomatic and humanitarian tasks.

TELECOMMUNICATIONS

Communications technology has played a significant role in Canada's global connections. The innovation involved in Canada's communications technology is undoubtedly related to Canada's vast land size and the need to be connected throughout the country. Many advances and contributions to world telecommunications have their roots in Canada—for instance, wireless telegraphy (radio), video and audio transmissions, and the invention of the telephone by Alexander Graham Bell. In 1972, the Canadian Broadcasting Corporation, built the first domestic satellite in the world (Anik A1), creating the first national satellite television system on Earth. This marked the first time Canada had ever received live television broadcasts. Canadians were among the first to use wireless technologies, and the use of such technologies developed and grew beyond that of any other area in the world. At present, many Canadian companies are involved in making significant contributions to Internet technology.

HUMANITARIAN AID

The Canadian government established the Canadian International Development Agency (CIDA) to help people in regions of the world that have suffered hardships such as disease and famine. The aims of CIDA are twofold: to promote sustainable activity and development and to assist areas of the world that require humanitarian assistance. While operating in different countries, CIDA seeks to develop programs and start projects that assist the citizens of particular communities. As a result, CIDA partners alongside a number of groups and organizations that include governments and non-governmental organizations, such as the Red Cross, churches, schools, and volunteers.

ARTS

A vast and exceptionally talented number of artists and artistic works have emerged from Canada. Artistic contributions by Canadians include offerings in music, dance, literature and poetry, artwork, and entertainment. Many Canadian performers participate in productions worldwide, and cities such as Montreal, Toronto, and Vancouver have large entertainment industries. Canadian artistic groups and works, such as those involved in music, theatre, dance, artwork, and sculpture, often travel throughout the world.

3.1.3   explain how Canada's natural systems form part of global natural systems

NATURAL SYSTEMS IN CANADA

Canada's natural systems form part of larger global natural systems that exist throughout the world and influence the unique nature of the environment. Powerful and dynamic (constantly changing) global systems impact the makeup and functioning of Canada's natural systems—that is, the atmosphere, the biosphere, the lithosphere, and the hydrosphere. These four spheres are layers that exist around Earth's core and interact to shape Earth's complex natural systems, which all living beings depend upon for survival.

Patterns of weather in Canada are connected to a constantly changing global climate system that is formed by the influence of the atmosphere, differences in Earth's landforms, and the circulation of ocean waters. For example, six huge and constantly moving air masses, which exist high over the atmosphere and stretch a distance of thousands of kilometres, influence Canada's daily weather. Continental arctic air that originates in Siberia may blow over the North Pole to Canada, influencing climate in Canada's biomes.

The global climate system influences smaller regional climate systems throughout the world, including those in Canada. These regional climate systems are the key factor in determining the nature of local ecosystems and the biomes of which they are a part. Thus, the location patterns of Canada's biomes and other biomes throughout the world are strongly influenced by the global climate system. When viewing maps of Earth's major biomes, they appear geographically as broad bands. These bands of global biomes correspond to zones of latitude throughout the world. Therefore, the specific types of plants that grow in each biome result from the influence of landforms and climates unique to those regions. Each of the world's biomes, including Canada's biomes, have a unique combination of characteristics that are shaped by Earth's natural systems.

Natural systems involving Earth's lithosphere influence a process called plate tectonics, which forms mountains that exist in Canada as well as throughout the world. Earth's lithosphere is thinnest under the oceans and thickest under the continents. The lithosphere is broken into a number of crustal plates that move very slowly upon Earth's underlying mantle. This movement either pushes the crustal plates together or pulls them apart. When plates collide, rocks crumple and form mountains. When one plate grinds into another and slides above it, massive tension builds in the rocks of the crust, and volcanic eruptions and earthquakes occur. Thus, earthquakes and volcanic activity are connected to areas where the edges of plates meet. The pattern of earthquakes and volcanic activity that occurs around the edge of the Pacific Ocean is referred to by geographers as the Ring of Fire. Most of the volcanic and earthquake activity that affects Canada occurs along the edges of Earth's crustal plates—for example, those of the Ring of Fire. Studying volcanic and earthquake activity helps geographers to understand how these processes shape Canada's unique geography and dynamic landforms.

Canada's natural systems are interconnected to larger global systems of nature. Geographic factors and processes that exist throughout the world contribute to the unique nature of Canada's biomes and influence Canadian's daily lives.

3.2.1   compare Canada's approaches to specific concerns with the approaches of other nations

CANADA'S APPROACHES TO ENVIRONMENTAL CONCERNS

ENVIRONMENTAL CHALLENGES

Canada and other nations face specific environmental concerns that affect natural systems globally. Canada's ecozones, like those throughout the world, are fragile natural environments. Some of the specific concerns that affect Earth's ecozones involve loss of species, deforestation, pesticide use, and cross-border pollution. The approaches and endeavors that Canada makes in addressing these environmental concerns can be compared to those that are made by other nations.

PESTICIDE USE

Changes to agricultural technology since the 1950s have led to advanced machinery, chemicals, and improved seed yields that have benefitted society by increasing the amount of food that farms in Canada and the world can produce. However, concerns have been raised about the possible effects on natural systems and human health from the use of hundreds of pesticides. In response to these concerns, the government has banned some extremely toxic pesticides and further limited pesticide use in Canada with a number of government acts. For example, the Canadian Environmental Protection Act (1999) serves to protect Canada's natural systems and human health while supporting pollution prevention and sustainable development of the environment. In Quebec, a province-wide ban exists on the residential use of weed-killing pesticides, as their use was felt to be unnecessary and for cosmetic purposes only. Other provinces are discussing similar action. Pesticides are used commonly around the world. Have other nations limited or banned pesticide use?

SPECIES LOSS

Within Canada's ecozones, several factors, such as pollution, rising temperatures from global warming, and overfishing, have contributed to species loss. For example, sea otters that live along British Columbia's coastline have been deemed a threatened species, in part because of over-hunting for their fur and also because of pollution from economic activities within Canada's ecozones that affect wildlife habitats. This also impacts Aboriginal communities that depend upon wildlife as part of their traditional way of life. Large numbers of animals have become extinct, extirpated (extinct in Canada), endangered, or threatened in the Prairie ecozone as a result of the loss of their natural grassland and wetland habitats because of agricultural activities. In order to address the issue of species loss in Canada, the Species at Risk Act (SARA) was created and became law in 2003 to prevent species from becoming extinct and to protect species and their habitats that are threatened with becoming endangered. Under the act, it is illegal to harm any species listed on the act or to destroy critical habitats. Additionally, other laws and programs are upheld by Canada's provincial and territorial governments to conserve and protect Canadian wildlife and their habitats. The success of these endeavors depends upon a combined effort of government, citizens, and industry. What measures have other nations taken to protect their environments from species loss?

DEFORESTATION

In order for Earth's forests to maintain sustainability, they need to be properly managed and cared for. Deforestation throughout the world is influenced by government policies toward forest reserves and how those forests will be used. Although many governments promote conservation of forests, policies have not always promoted sustainable forest practices. In Canada, most of the forested lands are publicly owned and controlled by the government (an exception is much larger private ownership in the Atlantic Maritime ecozone). The government leases large areas of forested land to forestry companies in order to produce lumber and wood products. In order to address environmental issues and protect the sustainability of Canada's forests, Canada has developed initiatives to address deforestation issues. For example, clear-cutting has raised a number of environmental concerns about forest sustainability. Soil erosion and barren, desert-like conditions can occur where clear-cutting takes place, as erosion can deplete the soil of nutrients and prevent new growth. Laws and regulations have been developed to work toward the sustainability of the forests, and in Ontario, forest management plans are legislated. Governments require twenty-year plans including specific goals and objectives from forestry companies to protect the forests from depletion and to preserve the wildlife habitats that exist within the forest ecosystems.

COMPARING CANADA AND OTHER NATIONS

Your studies will provide you with the opportunity to gather information pertaining to specific environmental concerns, such as deforestation, cross-border pollution, and pesticide use in Canada, and compare Canada's approach to that of other nations. What are the main factors that influence and contribute to these specific concerns in Canada and other countries? What initiatives or measures have been taken in response to environmental concerns in Canada and other nations, and how does Canada compare to other nations in terms of providing long-term solutions to environmental concerns?

3.2.2   evaluate Canada's participation in organizations that deal with global issues

CANADA'S PARTICIPATION IN GLOBAL ORGANIZATIONS

Canada takes part in a number of organizations that deal with global issues, such as human rights, global warming, and biodiversity. In participating in these organizations, Canada seeks to assist the global community in matters concerning the health, welfare, and human rights of people throughout the world and the sustainability of Earth's global natural systems.

One organization that Canada participates in is the United Nations, whose goals include supporting the protection of human rights and the sustainability of the environment. Canada participates in UN councils that seek to protect human rights, and Canada's early participation included drafting the Declaration of Human Rights more than fifty years ago. The United Nations Environment Programme (UNEP) is an entity of the United Nations that is involved in addressing environmental issues affecting Earth, both globally and regionally. Canada is presently a member state of the governing council of the United Nations Environment Programme, which reviews the global environment and brings emerging issues, such as global warming, to the awareness of governments and the international community. A number of international non-governmental organizations also seek solutions to global issues, such as those involving human rights and the sustainability of wildlife habitats. Some examples of non-governmental organizations are Oxfam and the World Wildlife Fund.

The support and respect for human rights and the quality of Earth's environment are matters of great importance to the global community. Some questions to include in your evaluation of Canada's participation in organizations that deal with global issues could include the following:

• What organizations of this nature does Canada participate in? Why?

• How does Canada play a role in these organizations?

• In what ways does Canada contribute to and support solutions to global issues?

• How can Canadians as global citizens improve the circumstances for other people in the world and the sustainability of the environment?

3.2.3   analyze the global distribution of selected commodities and determine Canada's share of each

THE GLOBAL DISTRIBUTION OF SELECTED COMMODITIES

Canada is known around the world as a country that has an abundance of natural resources and actively pursues resource development. Canada also plays a significant role in the global production of forest and agricultural products and the manufacture of goods and services. Analyzing the global distribution of selected commodities will lead to conclusions that can be made to help determine Canada's share of each.

Canada has a wealth of mineral and fuel deposits. Canada has the second largest oil reserves in the world; however, Canada is not the second largest oil producer. Some countries with smaller oil reserves produce more oil. The majority of the world's oil reserves are located in the Middle East.

Canada is also a top producer of a number of minerals. More than one-third of the potash mined globally comes from Canada, which accounts for nearly 35% of the world's supply. Canada is also the second largest world producer of uranium (approximately 30% of the world's supply), and Canada is ranked fourth in diamond production after Botswana, Russia, and Namibia.

Forests cover half of Canada's land area, and of those forested lands, 57% are considered to be of commercial forest value. Canada's boreal forest ecozone is part of Earth's largest ecozone area. Globally, Canada has the second largest commercial softwood forest in the world, with only Russia's being larger. Canada is a top producer of forest products, including furniture and newsprint.

Can connections be made between Canada's share of the global distribution of particular commodities and the economic activity and production of manufactured goods and services within Canada?

3.2.4   summarize ways in which the economies of Canada and the rest of the world are interdependent

CANADA'S ECONOMY AND THE WORLD

Canada's economy is based on goods and services that are produced in Canada. These goods and services are either used nationally or traded to other countries in order to produce a profit. The economies of Canada and other countries are interdependent because of a number of factors.

Many countries depend on trading relationships in order to benefit their economy and well-being. Canada depends on the export of Canadian resources (e.g., oil), goods (e.g., furniture), and services (e.g., financial) to other countries in order to gain the funds that are necessary to pay for the import of resources, goods, and services that the country requires. Like many other nations, Canada imports a vast array of natural resources (e.g., fruit from South America), manufactured goods, (e.g., electronics from Japan and Mexico), and services (e.g., entertainment-related services from the United States) from many countries in the world.

Canada's economy is interdependent with the economic trading needs and exports of other countries. Economic interdependence between Canada and other countries has emerged over the last century as a result of the need for resources or goods that cannot be derived or produced locally. Technologically, advanced forms of transportation (refrigeration, quantities of goods that can be transported), decreased travel time, and high-tech communications have served to link countries more closely. Global relationships have formed from increasing economic and social interactions between countries throughout the world—this is known as **globalization**.

As a consequence of global economic interdependency among countries, when one or more countries experience an economic boom or downturn, a ripple effect can sometimes occur. Thus, Canada's economy, like those of other countries, can be influenced to an extent by the economic circumstances of other countries. The greater the amount of trade activity that one country experiences with another country, the greater the possibility that the country's economy can be affected by economic circumstances within the other country.

A favourable balance of trade has been experienced by Canada in recent years. Canada participates actively in trade with many countries from around the world. The United States is Canada's largest trading partner. Canadian policies continue to pursue new export possibilities, economic opportunities, and trade relationships in the ever-changing global market.

3.2.5 evaluate the importance of tourism to Canada's economic development

TOURISM AND CANADA'S ECONOMIC DEVELOPMENT

Canada is a popular destination for many travellers, and tourism is of great importance to Canada's economy. Many tourist activities in Canada are for purposes of leisure and recreation, while some activities may also coincide with educational and business purposes. Canada's diverse and scenic landscapes from coast to coast offer tourists many exceptional sites, attractions, and parks featuring the nation's natural systems. Additionally, Canada's urban and rural centers offer a wealth of cultural and entertainment venues that feature Canada's human systems.

The tourism industry in Canada attracts thousands of travellers to Canada each year. Additionally, many Canadians travel to destinations within the country (domestic travel), which also boosts the amount of wealth created through tourism. Within the Mixedwood Plains ecozone are venues and sites that are visited by countless international travellers and Canadians throughout the year—for example, the CN Tower in Toronto; Wonderland, which is located north of Toronto in Maple, Niagara Falls; the Parliament Buildings in Ottawa; picturesque old Quebec City; and the Olympic Park complex in Montreal. These are only a few of the countless sites that are frequently visited by tourists. Additionally, park and forestry-related tourism in the ecozone, such as camping, produces tremendous amounts of revenue each year.

Tourism benefits the economy: wherever tourism occurs in Canada, the economy benefits. As a result, the importance of tourism to Canada's economy is immense. Tourism boosts local economies by bringing money into population centres, which influences the growth and prosperity of related service industries, such as hotels and restaurants. A **multiplier effect** occurs as money spreads through the community and further regional and national income can be gained. As jobs and services are created to support tourism, communities develop and prosper economically through tourist-related industries, such as tour operators. The government uses advertising to encourage international visitors to travel to Canada, and Canadians to travel within the country. Canadians also enjoy international travel to many foreign destinations, which then benefits the economies of other countries.

3.3.1 compare, in terms of resource use and consumption, the "ecological footprint" of an average Canadian with that of an average citizen in a developing country

ECOLOGICAL FOOTPRINTS

An ecological footprint is a measurement in hectares that calculates the amount of land and Earth's natural resources that are required to support the lifestyle of a nation or an individual. Factors such as transportation, water, and space required for work and living are used to calculate the footprints. What are other factors used to determine ecological footprints?

The calculated ecological footprint of Canada is comparatively larger than that of an average citizen in a developing country. Comparing these differing ecological footprints can educate you about your own lifestyle choices and you can make daily choices that can better ensure the sustainable use of natural resources.

Some questions to consider when comparing the ecological footprint of an average Canadian with that of an average citizen in a developing country are as follows:

• What different resources do Canadians and citizens that live in developing countries use? To what extent?

• What can be done to help developing countries that may not have adequate resources to contribute toward their quality of life?

- Are people's choices for resource use and consumption contributing to environmental sustainability of natural systems and the quality of life for future generations of Canadians?

- How can individuals and groups (e.g., citizens and city planners) try to lower the Canadian ecological footprint in order to help develop sustainable communities?

3.3.2   produce a set of guidelines for developing a solution to a global geographic or environmental issue

DEVELOPING A SOLUTION TO A GLOBAL, GEOGRAPHIC, OR ENVIRONMENTAL ISSUE

Geography involves connections between natural and human systems and understanding how people interact with Earth's environment. Many global, geographic, or environmental issues involve the impact and impressions that human activities, such as settlement, logging, mining, and waste disposal, have on Earth's global systems.

Geographic guidelines can form an outline that will serve as a geographic tool of inquiry to use in considering options, developing solutions, and determining short-term and long-term consequences of these solutions to a global geographic or environmental issue.

You can use a wide range of ideas, techniques, and tools to study and solve global geographic and environmental issues affecting Earth.

Geographic inquiry is one method that can be used to produce your guidelines. An example of information to consider in producing guidelines to global, geographic, or environmental issues is as follows.

First, an issue needs to be identified. Brainstorming questions pertaining to the issue can help shape a focus question on which the guidelines can be based. Next, gather information, research, and other forms of data, such as maps and graphs, pertaining to the focus question from a wide variety of primary and secondary sources. Remember to consider different points of view and any bias that may exist in information that is gathered. An environmental assessment would be very valuable in providing hands-on information that can influence the development of possible solutions. Also, is there an allowance for public input by concerned students or citizens about the issue?

Analyze and compare pieces of information. Focus on interconnections and dependencies between human and natural systems—people, wildlife, economic activities, and the natural environment (use webs, charts, and other visual organizers). Synthesize the data by creating new solutions or modifying those that exist. Consider different perspectives and utilize the most accurate and relevant ideas in developing solutions.

Each solution that is developed will require that possible consequences be suggested, tested, and evaluated as to whether these solutions will be feasible, dependable, and long-lasting. Expand upon the formation of solutions to a global, geographical, or environmental issue by communicating your solutions to your class, applicable parties, or government. Being global citizens can involve actively communicating geographic solutions to issues. Actions that you take can have important long-term environmental benefits and make Earth more sustainable for generations to come.

What guidelines can you create in developing solutions to global, geographic, or environmental issues?

PRACTICE QUESTIONS—GLOBAL CONNECTIONS

1. Which of the following countries is **not** a member of the North American Free Trade Agreement (NAFTA)?
   A. Mexico
   B. Canada
   C. Great Britain
   D. United States

2. The **most likely** reason that Canada was on the forefront of creating communication technologies is that
   A. Canadian universities offered top technological training
   B. Canada benefited from the United State's role in communications development
   C. Canadian secondary industries depended on developing communication technologies
   D. Canada's vast land size created the need to unite the country through communications

3. The process of plate tectonics has the **least** impact on Earth's
   A. lithosphere
   B. atmosphere
   C. human systems
   D. natural systems

4. In which parts of the world is Earth's crust **thinnest**?
   A. At the North and South Poles
   B. Beneath the continents
   C. Under the oceans
   D. At the equator

5. When an animal species ceases to exist in Canada but still lives in another area of the world, that animal species is referred to as
   A. endangered
   B. threatened
   C. extirpated
   D. extinct

6. Which of the following statements does **not** describe a reason that Canada participates in organizations that deal with global issues?

   A. Canada supports the protection of human rights.

   B. Canada is actively involved in resource development.

   C. Organizations such as these address issues involving human systems.

   D. Canada can gain financially from participation in these organizations.

7. Which of the following products could Canada **most likely** become a large manufacturer and exporter of in the next decade?

   A. Cellphones

   B. Potato chips

   C. Leather bags

   D. Diamond rings

8. Canada's **main** food imports include those fruits and vegetables that

   A. are not frequently eaten by Canadians

   B. are grown in warmer climates

   C. do not require refrigeration

   D. are processed and canned

9. Canada's tourism industry is **mainly** what type of industry?

   A. Primary

   B. Secondary

   C. Tertiary

   D. Quaternary

Use the following information to answer the next question.

The calculated ecological footprint for Canada is considerably larger than that of the world average and larger still than that of developing nations in the world.

10. When planners and geographers try to design local communities in Canada in ways that reduce their ecological footprint, they are **most likely** trying to balance

   A. global resource needs versus the sustainability of global natural systems

   B. economic development needs versus the sustainability of communities

   C. environmental needs versus the sustainability of human systems

   D. human needs versus the sustainability of natural systems

ANSWERS AND SOLUTIONS—PRACTICE QUESTIONS

1. C	3. B	5. C	7. D	9. C
2. D	4. C	6. D	8. B	10. D

1. C

Great Britain is not a member of NAFTA.

2. D

Canada's large land size created the need to unite the country through communications.

3. B

The process of plate movement leads to earthquakes and volcanic activity. The atmosphere would not sustain long-term effects from such activity.

The lithosphere contains Earth's natural and human systems, which would be impacted by earthquakes and volcanic activity. Earthquakes and volcanic activity can have serious effects on Earth's human systems—for example, loss of life and damage to transportation systems. Earthquakes and volcanic activity can also have long-term effects on Earth's natural systems—for example, the formation of mountain ranges.

4. C

Earth's crust is thinnest under the oceans.

5. C

Animal species that cease to exist in Canada but do exist in another part of the world are referred to as extirpated.

Animals that are endangered could become extirpated or extinct if they are not protected. Animals that are threatened are at risk of becoming endangered. Animals that are extinct do not live anywhere in the world.

6. D

In supporting organizations that deal with global issues, the welfare of humans or the environment are of prime importance. Profiting financially from these endeavors would most likely not be a reason for Canada's participation in such groups.

Canada is actively involved in resource development through its industries in the country. Canada supports the protection of human rights in the world. Organizations that deal with global issues do address issues involving the world's human and natural systems.

7. D

Canada is ranked fourth in the world in diamond production, and a number of diamond mines now exist in parts of Canada. Thus, it would be a reasonable conclusion that Canada could become a large manufacturer and exporter of diamond jewelry.

Many cellphones that Canadians use are foreign-made. Only 7% of Canada's lands are capable of sustaining potato crop production. Canada would not necessarily become a large producer of leather bags during the next decade.

8. B

Canada's main food imports include fruits and vegetables that are grown in warmer climates.

Canada's main food imports do not include foods that are not frequently eaten by Canadians. If there was no demand for these foods, they would not be a top import. Canada's main food imports do not necessarily include foods that are processed and canned. Canada's main food imports do include fruits and vegetables that may require refrigeration.

9. C

Tertiary industries provide services to Canadians. Tourism is a tertiary industry that provides travel services.

Primary industries are those that involve deriving or harvesting a natural resource from the environment—for example, farming and forestry are primary industries. Secondary industry mainly involves manufacturing. Quaternary industries are those involved with creating technology, ideas, and knowledge.

10. D

Community planners are most likely trying to balance human needs versus the sustainability of natural systems. Community planners are most likely trying to balance the needs of people that live in their local communities with protecting and preserving Earth's natural systems for future generations.

UNIT TEST—GLOBAL CONNECTIONS

1. Lowering atmospheric energy emissions is the primary goal of

   A. NAFTA

   B. La Francophonie

   C. the Kyoto Protocol

   D. the United Nations Environment Programme

Use the following information to answer the next question.

> In 2002, the United States imposed a tariff of 27% on Canadian softwood lumber.

2. Which of the following statements **most likely** reflects a consequence that occurred as a result of the given American action?

   A. In the United States, forestry product sales were protected, but a significant number of forestry workers lost their jobs.

   B. The economies of British Columbia, Saskatchewan, and Ontario were heavily impacted.

   C. The United States was able to discourage the import of foreign lumber products.

   D. The main intent of NAFTA was followed.

3. Lester B. Pearson contributed to the establishment of

   A. the North Atlantic Treaty Organization and the Asia-Pacific Economic Cooperative

   B. the North America Free Trade Agreement and the United Nations

   C. the United Nations and the North Atlantic Treaty Organization

   D. the Kyoto Protocol and the United Nations

4. The Canadian International Development Agency (CIDA) was formed in order to promote __*i*__ and offer __*ii*__ to people in areas of the world in need. The given statement is completed by the information in which of the following rows?

Row	*i*	*ii*
A.	sustainable development	humanitarian aid
B.	economic stability	agricultural technology
C.	peace	trading rights
D.	democracy	food, clothing, and shelter

5. The outer edge of British Columbia that extends under the ocean's surface is commonly referred to as
   A. a tectonic plate
   B. a continental shelf
   C. Earth's lithosphere
   D. Earth's underlying mantle

6. The **main** reason that earthquakes and volcanic activity occur along the Ring of Fire is
   A. global weather patterns
   B. human economic activity
   C. the movement of tectonic plates
   D. the location of the continental shelf

7. The growth of populations and the need for land for settlement in some developing countries has led to the depletion of which of the following natural resources?
   A. Fertile soils
   B. Livestock
   C. Minerals
   D. Forests

8. Which of the following ecozones has **most likely** experienced the greatest decrease in the amount of pesticide use?
   A. Boreal Plains
   B. Boreal Shield
   C. Atlantic Maritime
   D. Mixedwood Plains

9. Which of the following groups is a governmental organization that deals with global issues?
   A. Oxfam
   B. NAFTA
   C. United Nations
   D. World Wildlife Fund

Use the following information to answer the next question.

Canada participates in organizations that promote the sustainability of Earth's natural systems.

10. To "promote the sustainability of Earth's natural systems" means to
   A. not waste any leftover resources
   B. ensure that society has a good quality of life
   C. protect the environment by conserving resources
   D. create circumstances so that resources can last into the future

11. Which of the following phrases offers the **best** definition of "forests of commercial value"?
   A. Forests that can be leased or sold to other countries
   B. Forests that produce trees that can be harvested by clear-cutting
   C. Forests that produce wood that can be used in product manufacturing
   D. Forests of thick, dense trees that include a dense and vibrant undergrowth of vegetation

12. The **main** reason that Canada is a leading exporter of forest products is that
   A. most countries in the world need forest products from Canada
   B. Canada has vast amounts of land that contains commercial forest value
   C. Canadians have less need of wood and paper products compared to other countries in the world
   D. the United States agreed to pay back financial duties collected during the NAFTA softwood lumber dispute

13. Although import substitution would ensure more Canadian jobs and increase the amount of Canadian goods grown and consumed nationally (e.g, vegetables and fruits), one major drawback is that
   A. Canada would lose its relationships with its trading partners
   B. Canada would have to increase the use of pesticides
   C. Canadians would lack variety in their diets
   D. Canadians may suffer health-related issues

Use the following information to answer the next question.

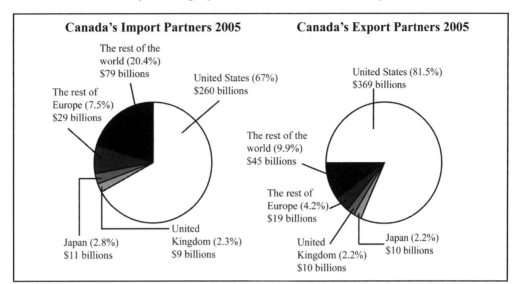

14. Which of the following conclusions can **most likely** be made from the information on the given pie graphs?

   A. The United States experienced a favourable balance of trade with Canada.

   B. The United Kingdom will become a larger trading partner to Canada in the future.

   C. Canada exported a smaller-valued amount of goods to Japan than it imported from Japan.

   D. The value of goods sent to Canada's second largest export market was nearly the same as the value of goods sent to Canada's largest export market.

Use the following information to answer the next question.

Sarah and her family visted a particular Canadian city to learn more about the National Gallery of Canada.

15. Sarah and her family **most likely** visited

   A. Niagara Falls

   B. Montreal

   C. Toronto

   D. Ottawa

Use the following information to answer the next question.

Renata and her family live in Kitchener. They have decided to take a trip to Hamilton, Ontario, where they will stay for one week with relatives. Then they will travel to Buffalo, New York, where they will stay for one week in a hotel while they hike in the surrounding areas and sightsee.

16. As a result of the family's vacation plans,

   A. both the economies of Canada and the United States benefit, but the Canadian economy benefits more

   B. both the economies of Canada and the United States benefit, but the American economy benefits more

   C. only the economy of the United States benefits

   D. only the economy of Canada benefits

17. The measure of the amount of land necessary to support the lifestyle of people living in Canada or other countries is known as

   A. the Kyoto measure

   B. the longevity index

   C. an economic forecast

   D. an ecological footprint

18. All of the following activities will not contribute to lowering Canadians' ecological footprints **except**

   A. walking instead of driving whenever possible

   B. utilizing disposable containers

   C. using high-energy appliances

   D. buying non-recyclable items

19. In terms of developing a solution to an environmental issue, geographic guidelines can serve as

   A. a summary of the issue

   B. an outline of how to proceed

   C. a collection of public input and ideas

   D. a sample of how other environmental issues were solved

20. Which of the following factors most likely has the least influence on the large size of some countries' ecological footprints in comparison to the small size of some countries' ecological footprints?

   A. Industrial activity

   B. Land size of the country

   C. Space used for human activity

   D. Availability of natural resources

ANSWERS AND SOLUTIONS—UNIT TEST

1. C	5. B	9. C	13. A	17. D
2. C	6. C	10. D	14. C	18. A
3. C	7. D	11. C	15. D	19. B
4. A	8. D	12. B	16. B	20. B

1. C

The primary goal of the Kyoto Protocol is to limit energy emissions and thus lower the production of greenhouse gases.

NAFTA was signed in order to promote and allow tariff-free trade. La Francophonie serves to support a number of initiatives involving linguistic and cultural diversity, peace, human rights, democracy, education and research, and cooperation toward sustainable development. The United Nations Environment Programme (UNEP) addresses a number of environmental issues affecting Earth.

2. C

The United States was able to discourage the import of Canadian softwood lumber by placing tariffs on it.

In the United States, forestry products and jobs were protected. The main intent of NAFTA is to encourage and allow tariff-free trade. This intent was not adhered to when the United States placed a 27% tariff on Canadian softwood lumber. The economies of British Columbia, Ontario, and Quebec were heavily impacted.

3. C

Lester B. Pearson contributed to the establishment of the United Nations and NATO following the Second World War.

Lester B. Pearson was not involved in the establishment of the North American Free Trade Agreement, the Asia-Pacific Economic Cooperative, or the Kyoto Protocol.

4. A

CIDA was formed in order to provide humanitarian aid and promote sustainable development for people of the world who have suffered hardships.

Economic stability and agricultural technology are issues that are part of sustainable development. The main purpose of CIDA is not to provide trading rights.

5. B

The outer edge of British Columbia that extends under the ocean's surface is commonly referred to as a continental shelf.

It is not commonly referred to as a tectonic plate, Earth's lithosphere, or Earth's underlying mantle.

6. C

Plate tectonics is responsible for most earthquakes and volcanic activity along the Ring of Fire.

Global weather patterns, human economic activity, and the location of the continental shelf are not responsible for earthquakes and volcanic activity.

7. D

Growing populations and the need for land for settlement in some of developing countries has led to the depletion of forests. This has resulted from the need to clear the land for homes.

Soil in areas of settlement would not necessarily have been favourable for farming. Settlement has not led to the depletion of minerals or livestock.

8. D

The Mixedwood Plains contains Canada's largest population base and the majority of Canada's fertile soils, which are used for a great deal of farm production. Thus, the Mixedwood Plains ecozone most likely has experienced the greatest reduction in pesticide use.

Agriculture is much more limited in the Boreal Plains ecozone than in the Mixedwood Plains ecozone. Lands of the Boreal Shield are mainly forest-covered. The Atlantic Maritime ecozone contains agricultural lands and most likely has experienced some reduction in pesticide use, but not to the extent of the Mixedwood Plains ecozone.

9. C

The United Nations is an international organization that was founded in 1945 to promote cooperation, peace, and security in the world. The UN includes membership by 192 countries worldwide, including Canada.

Oxfam is a non-governmental organization. The North American Free Trade Agreement was formed between Canada, the United States, and Mexico in order to promote tariff-free trade in North America. It is an agreement that pertains to North America. The World Wildlife fund is a non-governmental organization.

10. D

Sustainability requires both the conservation of resources and ensuring that resources can renew themselves or be replaced by other resources (preservation). Creating these circumstances can promote a sustainable resource system that will last for future generations.

Not wasting leftover resources is part of conserving resources, which influences the sustainability of Earth's natural systems. Sustainability also involves preserving natural resources. Promoting the sustainability of Earth's natural systems ensures the quality of life for future generations.

11. C

Forests of commercial value produce wood that can be used in product manufacturing.

Forests of commercial value do not necessarily have to be harvested by clear-cutting and are not defined as forests that are sold or leased to other countries. Forests of thick and dense trees that include a dense and vibrant undergrowth of vegetation more accurately describes a rainforest.

12. B

The main reason that Canada is a leading exporter of forest products is because Canada contains vast areas of forested land, the majority of which is considered to be of commercial value.

Most countries in the world do not require forest products specifically from Canada. The fact that the United States agreed to pay back duties collected during the NAFTA softwood lumber dispute is not the main reason why Canada is a leading exporter of forest products. Canadians do not have less need of wood and paper products compared to other countries in the world.

13. A

Canada would lose its relationships with its trading partners because of import substitution, and this may isolate Canada from the benefit of global interconnections that exist between countries in the world.

The lack of variety in Canadians' diets would not be a major drawback to import substitution. Canada would not necessarily have to increase the use of pesticides because of import substitution. Canadians would not necessarily suffer health-related issues from import substitution.

14. C

Canada exported a smaller-valued amount of goods to Japan ($10 billion) than it imported from Japan ($11 billion).

Canada exported more goods to the United States in 2005 ($369 billion) than it received from the United States ($260 billion). Thus, Canada had a favourable balance of trade with the United States. The value of goods that Canada exported to Japan ($10 billion) was vastly smaller than the amount of goods that Canada exported to the United States ($369 billion). There is no evidence from the pie graphs that the United Kingdom will become a larger trading partner to Canada in the future. In 2005, Canada exported 2.2% of its exports to the United Kingdom and received 2.3% of its imports from the United Kingdom.

15. D

The National Gallery of Canada is located in Canada's national capital, Ottawa. The National Gallery of Canada is not located in Niagara Falls, Montreal, or Toronto.

16. B

Both economies benefit to differing extents. The American economy benefits more than the Canadian economy because Renata's family pays for a one-week hotel stay in Buffalo plus meals, and these meals would most likely be consumed in restaurants in Buffalo. This is compared to their stay with family in Hamilton. More money goes into the American economy than the Canadian economy as a result of their travel expenses.

17. D

An ecological footprint is the measure of the amount of land necessary to support either a person's lifestyle or the lifestyle within a country. Hectares are the unit of measurement used to measure an ecological footprint.

The Kyoto Protocol is an international treaty that seeks to limit environmental emissions and the production of greenhouse gases. The measure of the amount of land necessary to support the lifestyle of those within a country is not known as the longevity index. An economic forecast looks at a country's possible long-range economic growth.

18. A

Walking instead of driving whenever possible will serve to cut down on emissions and contribute to lowering people's ecological footprints.

Buying items that cannot be recycled, using high-energy appliances, and using disposable containers will not contribute to lowering Canadians' ecological footprints.

19. B

Geographic guidelines serve as an outline of how to proceed in order to develop a solution to an issue.

A geographic outline would not be a summary of the environmental issue, a collection of public input and ideas, or a sample of how other environmental issues were solved.

20. B

A larger land size does not necessarily mean that a county will have a larger ecological footprint.

Industrial activity and resource use would most likely influence the size of a country's ecological footprint. Availability of natural resources and the amount of space that is necessary for human activity would most likely influence the size of a country's ecological footprint.

NOTES

Understanding and Managing Change

UNDERSTANDING AND MANAGING CHANGE

Table of Correlations		
Specific Expectation	**Practice Questions**	**Unit Test Questions**
Students are expected to:		
4.1 *explain how natural and human systems change over time and from place to place*		
4.1.1 recognize the similarities among cultures and the need to respect cultural differences	2, 3, 4	
4.1.2 explain how selected factors cause change in human and natural systems		3, 4
4.1.3 identify and explain the factors influencing demographics and migration in Canada	1, 10	1, 2, 5, 6, 7, 8, 9
4.2 *predict how current or anticipated changes in the geography of Canada will affect the country's future economic, social, and environmental well-being*		
4.2.1 anlayse different perspectives on a geographic issue and present arguments supporting a point of view	5, 8, 9	10, 11, 12, 13
4.2.2 predict the consequences of human activities on natural systems		14
4.2.3 analyse the positive and negative effects on people and the environment of the manufacturer, transportation to market, and consumption of selected products	6	15, 16, 17, 18
4.3 *explain how global economic and environmental factors affect individual choices*		
4.3.2 predict various global environmental changes and the impact they may have in the future on the occupation of Canadians in various sectors of the economy	7	

UNDERSTANDING AND MANAGING CHANGE

4.1.1   recognize the similarities among cultures and the need to respect cultural differences

DIVERSITY

Canada is home to an incredible variety of different cultures, with over 200 ethnic groups making up the population. People have come to live here from around the world and continue to come. Toronto, Canada's largest city, is proof of this: around half of Toronto's population consists of visible minorities.

Canada does not expect people to assimilate, that is, to adopt a uniform Canadian culture. Instead, Canada maintains an official policy of multiculturalism that encourages people to keep and celebrate their individual cultural backgrounds. Canada is often referred to as a cultural mosaic, where each culture contributes to the overall picture.

The word culture encompasses a wide variety of things: clothing, food, music, religious or spiritual beliefs, traditions, language, and so forth. Cultures from around the world have changed the way Canadians live, eat, and entertain themselves. When you visit a mall food court, you can order Japanese sushi, Mexican tacos, Greek souvlaki, Chinese rice or noodle meals, Italian pizza, American burgers, or Indian curry. You might have ethnic neighbourhoods in your hometown (Chinatown, Little Italy, etc.). You can attend—or participate in—a cultural festival, like Toronto's Caribana or Ottawa's Carnival of Cultures.

In short, Canada is a country where people from all over the world can live and work together in peace. Canadians have learned to respect, even celebrate, their cultural differences and to understand their similarities. No matter what their cultural background, people generally want the same things: to meet their basic needs, to be safe from crime and violence, to support and nurture their children, and to worship as they choose. In Canada, these wants and needs are recognized and protected by law.

Multiculturalism is not without its challenges, however. There are always those who choose to discriminate against persons of different cultures or ethnicities, although this is hardly unique to multicultural societies. On a more theoretical level, because of its policy of multiculturalism, it is difficult for Canada to pinpoint a national identity: what, if anything, defines Canadian culture? What, besides citizenship, makes someone Canadian? These questions are not easily answered; they are studied and debated in the media, in classrooms, in universities, and between individuals.

Overall, though, Canadians choose to celebrate their cultural diversity in spite of the challenges it presents. Multiculturalism provides countless opportunities to learn and grow as human beings.

4.1.2   explain how selected factors cause change in human and natural systems

CHANGE IN HUMAN AND NATURAL SYSTEMS

Whether human or natural, systems are rarely isolated from one another. Changes in one system almost always will affect other systems. Therefore, it is important to recognize how systems relate to one another and to be aware of the factors that cause change in them. A good example of how systems affect each other in Canada is in the development of oil resources, which has altered natural, local, provincial, federal, and even global systems.

THE OIL SANDS

Canada is a resource-rich nation, and in today's economy, few resources are more precious than oil. Canada's oil reserves are second only to those of Saudi Arabia; of those reserves, the vast majority lies in Alberta's oil sands. These sands contain an extremely heavy and thick form of crude oil called bitumen; the oil sands are often referred to as tar sands.

ECONOMIC CHANGES

Recovering this heavy oil is a difficult and costly process, so exploitation of the oil sands used to be limited. In recent years, though, oil costs have jumped to over USD $100 per barrel, making the development of the oil sands an extremely profitable venture. Investment has soared, so far totalling around 100 billion Canadian dollars. Alberta, already one of Canada's economically strongest provinces, stands to gain billions in royalties.

The economic impact of the oil sands goes beyond the energy sector. The bitumen needs to be recovered, refined, and transported to a variety of markets. This means that other industries—automotive, transportation, smelting, and so forth—benefit as well. People from all across Canada are finding employment in the oil sands; those people need homes, transportation, food, entertainment, and other services. This need creates even more jobs. Unemployment has gone down across the country, and that, at least in part, is due to the oil sands.

This growth has led to widespread labour shortages in other sectors, however. Investment in other sectors has declined also because individuals and companies choose to invest in lucrative oil sands projects. Conventional oil and gas, manufacturing, and agriculture are some of the sectors that have been hurt—all important areas in Ontario's economy. For residents of Alberta, the cost of living has increased sharply, as have real estate prices.

ENVIRONMENTAL CHANGES

The economy and the environment are arguably the two most important areas of concern for Canadians, so it is no surprise that the oil sands are a hot issue. Opinions vary widely as to the environmental impact of the oil sands projects.

To date, most of the bitumen has been extracted through surface mining. The top layer of soil is removed, and the bitumen-heavy sand lying relatively close to the surface is mined and taken to processing facilities. Because the surface soil and vegetation are stripped away, this process is often called strip mining. Much of the bitumen lies under boreal forest or peat wetlands, so surface mining is a potential danger to these natural systems.

The Alberta government claims that every effort is made to minimize the impact of oil sands development on the environment. It has passed strict laws regarding water use, emissions, and the reclamation of mined land. Reclamation, in this case, means restoring the land to allow the growth of new natural systems once the bitumen has been removed. Greenhouse gas emissions from the oil sands comprise about 3% of Canada's total. Furthermore, the government offers large monetary incentives for projects that are demonstrably environmentally sound.

Environmental organizations, such as Greenpeace, the World Wildlife Fund, and the Pembina Institute, are sharply critical of the way that the oil sands are being exploited. They claim that oil sands projects use an unsustainable level of water and that their activities threaten the Athabasca water table, which covers much of Alberta, Saskatchewan, and the Northwest Territories. Furthermore, the greenhouse gas emissions from the oil sands projects, while comprising about 3% of Canada's total, undermine our obligations to reduce emissions under the Kyoto protocols. Finally, they point out that wetlands cannot simply be restored after strip mining; wetlands are complex ecosystems that take hundreds or thousands of years to develop.

POLITICAL CHANGES

Although oil extraction is far easier and cheaper from oil wells in places like the Middle East, such regions are often politically unstable, hostile towards the United States, or simply geographically distant. Canada is a stable Western democracy, a capitalist nation that is both physically and culturally close to the United States. The vast majority of our oil production goes to the United States, but the recent economic growth of China and other Pacific Rim nations has led to a sharp increase in the demand for oil there as well. The oil sands, therefore, heighten Canada's importance in the world, both politically and economically.

A new set of issues and concerns from within Canada and from abroad has come along with this new importance, however. The governments of Canada and Alberta are under increased pressure to slow, or even stop, new investment in the oil sands. Some believe that the unchecked growth of oil sands investment is damaging Canada's overall economy; others have environmental concerns. Tension between the provinces is mounting as well; the government of Ontario in particular has been sharply critical of the impact of the oil sands on its key industries.

SOCIAL CHANGES

The unofficial capital of the oil sands is Fort McMurray. It has gone from a modest northern Alberta town to a municipal region nearing 100 000 people. This growth has placed incredible strain on local residents and municipal governments, who must struggle to house, feed, and provide infrastructure for so many new residents. Roads, sewers, utilities, hospitals, emergency services, and law enforcement services are not adequate to handle the influx, given how quickly it has occurred.

The oil sands boom has also proved a mixed blessing for the local First Nations. They, too, have shared in the economic windfall provided by the oil sands, but divisions within the community are growing. Some Aboriginals are concerned about the impact the boom is having on their traditional ways of life, especially on hunting and fishing. Others believe that the people of the First Nations have a role as caretakers of nature and are worried about the impact on the environment.

CAUSE AND EFFECT

Everything described above was caused, in essence, by one simple change: an increase in the global price of oil. Because the nations of the world are becoming increasingly interlinked, local changes can have huge effects. A forest fire in British Columbia can affect the cost of new homes in Winnipeg. A war in the Middle East can create jobs in Sudbury. A shift in international diplomacy might lower the cost of food at your local grocery store. What might a sharp decline in the price of oil do?

4.1.3   identify and explain the factors influencing demographics and migration in Canada

DEMOGRAPHICS AND MIGRATION IN CANADA

DEMOGRAPHY

Demography is the study of population statistics. For example, a demographer might study the population growth in a particular area, the average number of hospital visits per year, the average size of households in the area, and so forth. Demography provides important information to governments and other organizations. In Canada, a federal department called Statistics Canada is the primary body in charge of demography.

To collect information about the Canadian population, Statistics Canada conducts a census every five years. Each household in the country completes a detailed form designed to collect information on a wide variety of demographic statistics. Canadians have the option of completing their census over the Internet.

One of the most basic and important pieces of demographic data is population growth. Being able to anticipate population growth allows government bodies to plan infrastructure, change electoral districts to provide more accurate representation, set immigration targets, and make any number of other important decisions. Population growth is determined by four basic factors: birth rate, death rate, immigration, and emigration.

Simply put, the birth rate measures how many Canadians are born per year, and the death rate measures how many Canadians die per year. Birth rate and death rate are generally measured in persons per thousand. For example, the annual birth rate in Canada is about 10 births per thousand Canadians. By subtracting the death rate from the birth rate, demographers determine the natural increase rate of population growth. A low natural increase rate is one characteristic of a developed, industrialized nation or area. Some countries in the world actually have a negative natural increase rate: the population is shrinking over time.

The other two population growth factors are immigration and emigration. Immigration is when people come to an area from elsewhere; emigration is when people leave an area to go elsewhere.

POPULATION BREAKDOWN

Demographers often make graphical representations of populations. One of these is the population pyramid, where the population is divided by gender and then ranked by age. Since there tend to be somewhat fewer people at each age level, as such things as accidents and disease take their toll, the resulting shape is generally a pyramid.

Canada's population pyramid does not look pyramidal at all. Those of the baby boom generation, born not long after the Second World War, are currently in their late-forties to late-fifties. Right now, there are more people in that age category than in any other. Eventually, there will be more senior citizens in Canada than children, which may place a great strain on health care, pensions, and other services.

IMMIGRATION TO CANADA

Generally speaking, Canada wants immigrants to be able to support themselves when they come here. Citizenship and Immigration Canada (CIC), the department in charge of immigration, tests immigrants on their ability to be financially self-sufficient when they arrive. CIC breaks immigration down into four different areas: economic immigration, family immigration, refugees, and other.

Economic immigration is when people come to Canada to work. CIC assesses the skills of such immigrants to ensure that they will be able to find work in Canada, especially in the case of skilled workers. They look at things like proficiency in English or French, age, and pre-arrangement of employment. Economic immigration comprises about 60% of Canada's annual immigration.

Immigration can be expensive; often, only one person is able to come at first. Once that person is financially stable, he or she can apply to sponsor his or her family. This is called family immigration. Another form of family immigration is the adoption of children from other nations.

Refugees are persons who have had to flee their home nation because they are in danger of torture, unjust imprisonment, or death. They may be escaping from a brutal or unstable government, from war, or from a major natural disaster that makes daily life impossible. Although refugees often arrive in Canada with little or no ability to be financially self-sufficient, the government offers special programs to help them adjust.

IMMIGRATION CAUSES AND CONCERNS

People choose to leave their home countries for many different reasons: lack of work, religious or racial oppression, lack of personal freedoms, dissatisfaction with the government, overcrowding, natural disasters, and so forth. The factors that encourage people to decide to leave are called push factors.

Once people have decided to leave their home, they must decide where to go. The factors that encourage people to emigrate to a particular nation are that nation's pull factors. Canada has several pull factors: social, religious, and political freedoms; a stable government; a capitalist economy with a social safety net; strong educational systems; a tolerant society; and any number of other social, political, and economic factors.

This is not to say that it is always easy for immigrants to flourish in Canada. It can be difficult to adjust to an entirely new way of life while maintaining employment or pursuing an education. Because employment standards and educational curricula vary so widely around the world, immigrants often struggle to adapt. This can be especially hard on professionals, such as doctors and teachers, who discover that their credentials are not recognized in Canada. This means that some highly-educated individuals end up underemployed.

MIGRATION WITHIN CANADA

Canadians can move freely from one province or territory to another. Interprovincial migration is another area of interest for governments. In recent years, Alberta and British Columbia have received large influxes of people from other provinces. With the Maritime fishing industry in poor shape, many people from such provinces as Newfoundland and Labrador, Prince Edward Island, and New Brunswick have left in search of jobs. Since British Columbia's fishing industry is relatively strong, many choose to migrate there; others hope to benefit from Alberta's rapidly-growing oil industry.

4.2.1 analyse different perspectives on a geographic issue and present arguments supporting a point of view

DIFFERENT PERSPECTIVES ON GEOGRAPHIC ISSUES

Around 80% of Canadians live in cities, and the rate of urbanization is increasing over time. Growing cities often spread onto adjacent land, either directly or through the construction of suburbs. This phenomenon is called urban sprawl. Urban sprawl presents governments and citizens with a host of challenges: infrastructure creation and maintenance, loss of agricultural land, traffic congestion, and so forth. Opinions vary on how, and to what extent, cities should deal with urban sprawl.

Simply disallowing any new city growth is not an option. Economically, it is far less expensive to allocate new land to a city than it is to implement large-scale changes that reduce development. Also, many individuals prefer the suburban lifestyle with its increased privacy, greater living space, lower levels of noise and pollution, and so forth. Land developers, construction companies, tradespersons, real estate agents, and other organizations or individuals can make large profits from suburban development.

One of the key problems with urban sprawl is the resultant commute between the suburbs and the city. Roads must be built and maintained to support the traffic; the relatively long drives increase energy consumption, air pollution, and the risk of accidents. When suburban dwellers reach their destinations, they need places to park their cars, which means even less space in the city for residences.

Possible solutions:

- Mass transit reduces the number of vehicles on the road. Most large Canadian cities also have some form of rapid transit system (subways or above-ground railcars). If the transit system is well-run and convenient for commuters, it will reduce their reliance on automobiles.

- Another solution is to mix land use. This means building homes, offices, stores, schools, clinics, and other services near one another. That way, people can walk, instead of drive, to work, school, or shopping.

- Many businesses eliminate the need for commuting by allowing telecommuting. This is when employees work from home, using telephones, fax machines, or the Internet to connect with the workplace.

- City governments can increase living space by zoning high-density residential space: high-rise apartment buildings or condominiums, for example.

- Governments can restrict or disallow growth into certain areas. For example, the Ontario government has designated much of the area around Toronto as protected land.

While helpful, these solutions pose challenges of their own. For example, creating and maintaining a transit system is expensive. The need to limit urban sprawl must be balanced with economic reality. Municipal governments across Canada have chosen their own methods for addressing urban sprawl.

4.2.2   predict the consequences of human activities on natural systems

THE CONSEQUENCES OF HUMAN ACTIVITIES ON NATURAL SYSTEMS

THE CHALLENGES OF AGRICULTURE

About 7% of Canada's area is arable (suitable for crops). Canada is a large country, so 7% encompasses a lot of land. Canada has two main agricultural areas: the Prairies (southern Alberta, Saskatchewan, and Manitoba), and along the St. Lawrence River and into the Great Lakes region. These areas are devoted to raising crops and livestock, and provide Canadians with both food and economic opportunities.

Agriculture can be a lucrative business, but farmers must overcome several challenges to be successful. Their crops are vulnerable to a variety of natural hazards (such as floods or early frosts) or changes in weather patterns (such as periods of drought). Livestock, too, is vulnerable; diseases such as bovine spongiform encephalopathy (BSE, or mad cow disease) can threaten herds and cause health concerns for consumers. Farmers also face competition from large agribusinesses or from farmers in other countries.

To stay competitive, farmers must try to get the most out of their land while keeping their operating costs low. There are several strategies a farmer can use, but these strategies often impact the environment.

PESTICIDES

To maintain a healthy crop, farmers must eliminate insect pests that might eat the produce; they also must control weeds that compete with crops for soil resources. To do so, farmers use pesticides, which are products that kill harmful insects and plants. These products must be used with care, though; if pesticides enter a natural system, they can endanger plants, animals, and even humans. Responsible farmers are careful to ensure that pesticides do not contaminate nearby rivers or lakes.

PREVENTING SOIL DEPLETION

When crops grow, they extract nutrients from the soil. Over time, these nutrients are depleted, unless farmers take steps to restore them. One ecologically-friendly way to do so is to allow fields to lie fallow (unused) for a period of time. However, this means that the farmer is not receiving any immediate profit from that field.

Alternatively, farmers can practise crop rotation. For example, they can split their land into three portions and alternate their regular crop with a type of plant called a nitrogen fixer. Nitrogen fixers (such as beans or peas) release nitrogen, a key element for plant growth, into the soil. This is economically more beneficial for farmers than letting fields lie fallow.

Even crop rotation is not always sufficient to restore all the nutrients in the soil. To counteract soil depletion, and to increase the size of the harvest, farmers use fertilizers. Fertilizers are substances that contain plant nutrients; they come from natural or synthetic sources. Overuse of fertilizers can damage crops, so farmers are careful to use them in moderation. They must also take care not to let fertilizers contaminate natural systems and upset the balance of ecosystems. For example, fertilizers promote the growth of toxic algae in lakes, which can be dangerous for plants, animals, and people who rely on the lake for water.

PREVENTING SOIL EROSION

Erosion is when soil is lost because of such forces as wind or rain. When a crop is harvested or if livestock have eaten all the vegetation, the soil is left bare and vulnerable to erosion. During dry conditions, strong winds can carry away the fertile top layer of soil. In wet conditions, soil can be washed away by heavy rains or melting snow, often ending up as sediment in nearby rivers or lakes.
This is a problem not only because soil is lost, but because that soil is often contaminated with pesticides, fertilizers, or animal dung. All of these are harmful to the environment. Fortunately, there are farming practices and technologies that can help prevent soil erosion.

4.2.3 analyse the positive and negative effects on people and the environment of the manufacture, transportation to market, and consumption of selected products

EFFECTS OF MANUFACTURING, TRANSPORTATION, AND CONSUMPTION OF PRODUCTS

Canada is a relatively wealthy nation, and Canadians can get goods from all over the world. A Canadian might wake up in the morning, put on some clothes (sewn in India), grab a cup of coffee (from Columbian beans), hop in the car (designed in Germany, assembled in the U.S.), and drive to work. At the office, that Canadian might work on a computer (built from Japanese parts) and then go home to watch television (made in China).

Situations like the one given above are so common these days that Canadians rarely think about the origins of their products. Still, by the time any product is available for purchase, it has been designed, built (or harvested, sewn, etc.), and transported to Canada. So, who harvested that coffee? Who sewed those clothes? How much were the workers paid? How do they live? How did that computer get from Japan to your desktop?

These are not always easy questions for Canadians to ask; there simply is not enough time to research fully the origins and impact of every single product purchased. Nonetheless, consumers should be aware that every product has its own history. As an example, let's look at a common Canadian purchase: the banana. Bananas are among the most popular produce items sold at Canadian supermarkets, and the average Canadian consumes around 13 kilograms of bananas per year.

Virtually all bananas in Canada come from Latin American countries like Ecuador, Honduras, Panama, and Guatemala. Canada does not import them directly; the United States imports the bananas and then re-exports them to Canada. Bananas are not a very robust fruit, though; they bruise easily and are susceptible to pests and plant diseases. Therefore, special care is taken to protect them: pesticides are liberally applied as they grow, and the fruit is shipped in special refrigerated containers to prevent it from ripening too quickly.

THE BENEFITS

The primary benefits of the banana trade are economic. It generates sales of over $10 billion per year and provides jobs for millions of people: plantation workers, dock workers, freight handlers, ships' crews, truck drivers, and so forth. Bananas are a cash crop that provides a great deal of revenue to Latin American countries, and countries in Africa and Southeast Asia are starting their own banana production.

Socially, bananas have become a staple food item in Europe, the United States, and Canada, and are increasingly popular in Japan. Bananas are a healthy, convenient, and easily-digested tropical fruit with a low incidence of allergic reactions, which means they are suitable for all kinds of diets. Thus, bananas appear in packed lunches, baby food, dinners, and desserts all around the world.

THE COSTS

The primary costs of banana production are environmental and social. Banana producers are under pressure from supermarkets and consumers to provide a low-cost, high-quality fruit, and this has often come at the expense of the plantation workers and local ecosystems. Indeed, the history of banana production in Latin America is filled with widespread human rights abuses and environmental destruction.

In the past, the life of a plantation worker was characterized by starvation wages, unsafe working conditions, sexual harassment, job instability, anti-union practices, child labour, and excessive work hours. Plantations often sprayed toxic pesticides in areas where workers were present. In the 1980s, a common pesticide called Nemagon caused sterility in thousands of male plantation workers; more than 50 000 people have filed lawsuits.

Banana production has also damaged the environment. To establish a plantation, local vegetation is eliminated so that it will not compete with the banana plants for resources. Plantations tend to employ intensive agricultural practices, including frequent spraying of pesticides and fertilizer use. This leads to the contamination of local waterways (where people get drinking water and wash their clothes) and the depletion of the soil.

THE CHALLENGES

In the mid-1980s, banana producers came under increased scrutiny from ecologically-conscious consumers, the International Labour Organization of the United Nations, and various non-governmental organizations (NGOs) dedicated to social or environmental causes. Pressure from these groups has forced the major banana producers to improve their practices.

In recent years, the big banana producers have tried to improve their image by voluntarily applying environmental management and social accountability initiatives. For example, Chiquita has agreed to comply with the ISO-14001 environmental standard and the SA8000 social accountability standard.

It has also signed an agreement with the Sustainable Agriculture Network, an alliance of environmental NGOs led by the Rainforest Alliance. Dole, Chiquita's chief competitor, has taken similar steps in regards to their own plantation management.

Some groups are pleased that companies like Dole and Chiquita are mending their ways. Others accuse them of green-washing: hiding abuses behind a public façade of environmental and social consciousness. Still others point out that Dole and Chiquita only represent 50% of the world export market; human rights abuses and environmental damage are still the norm in many areas.

THE ALTERNATIVES

Some consumers do not want to buy products that, in their view, come from the exploitation of people and the environment. Those consumers may boycott such products, or they may ensure that the products they buy were produced ethically.

In recent years, two new options have become available for consumers: certified organic and fair-trade products. To be certified organic, a banana (or other type of produce) must have been grown according to strict rules regarding the use of natural fertilizers and pesticides, the conservation of water and soil, and the recycling of waste. A fair-trade label on a banana indicates that the plantation workers were paid enough to support themselves and that they were not subjected to any human rights abuses. Both certified organic and fair-trade bananas are more expensive than conventional bananas, but many consumers are happy to pay a premium to protect human beings and the environment from exploitation.

4.3.1   evaluate the impact of change on a selected planning project

IMPACT OF CHANGE ON A PLANNING PROJECT

Humans generate a lot of trash, especially humans living in industrialized nations. Getting rid of garbage is an age-old problem; people usually deal with trash by burying it, burning it, or dumping it in the water. In the 20th century, people became more aware of the environmental hazards these methods pose and started taking steps to make garbage disposal more efficient and environmentally safe.

LANDFILLS

Landfills are sites where trash is delivered, compacted, and stored, generally in large pits. In the past, abandoned quarries or mines served as landfills. While these may have been more or less convenient, they were not safe. When it rained, the water percolated down through the mass of garbage and became contaminated; this contaminated water is called leachate. Leachate would soak into the ground and mix with the groundwater.

Modern landfills use impermeable liners to prevent groundwater contamination. They also regularly cover the trash with earth, temporary blankets, or foam sealants that prevent odour and keep vermin away. Once a landfill is full, the land can be reclaimed by covering it with a layer of soil. Many golf courses and other recreational facilities are built on areas of reclaimed landfill.

INCINERATORS

Incinerators are facilities where waste is burned at very high temperatures. They reduce the amount of solid waste that must be disposed of, but they also pollute the air. Trash incineration can generate greenhouse gases, particularly carbon dioxide, and can also release tiny particles of toxic substances into the air.

Modern incinerators include a variety of technologies to prevent, or at least severely limit, air pollution, although disposal of the toxic ash is still a problem. Many incinerators are designed to generate power and heating from the combustion of waste. Incinerators use used extensively in various European countries, particularly Denmark and Sweden.

PLASMA ARC TECHNOLOGY

One promising technology for waste disposal is plasma arc gasification, where inert gases are vented through a powerful electrical arc. The gas reaches extremely high temperatures—as high as 14 000°C—and can break down most types of waste into component elements. The gases that are generated can be reclaimed as fuel, and the solid material is, for the most part, safe and recyclable.

The Canadian company Plasco Energy Group Inc. has pioneered the use of plasma arc gasification in its Trail Road facility in Ottawa. This is a demonstration facility that can handle up to 100 tonnes of unsorted waste per day. It focuses on reclaiming, rather than destroying, the material that passes through. Plasco claims that 99.8 percent of the waste is recovered as gas, water, and other useful materials. The released heat can be used as a power source; each tonne of waste is enough to power around 45 homes for a day.

The advantages to systems like Plasco's are numerous: a fraction of the waste remains; there is virtually no air pollution; power, water, and heat energy are generated; and useable gases, salt, and other materials are produced. Such systems also could reduce our reliance on non-renewable fossil fuels, such as coal. They use land far more efficiently: plasma arc gasification facilities can be located near or even within city limits. In fact, this is advantageous because it means less pollution is made getting trash to the facility.

Plasco is planning to build more facilities in Canada and the United States, as well as collaborating on a mixed waste-treatment facility in Wales. Other companies are constructing plasma arc gasification facilities around the world, some of which will be capable of processing thousands of tonnes per day. It is possible that sometime in the future people will be able to process more trash than they generate, not only keeping ahead of their own garbage, but eliminating what is sitting in landfills.

4.3.2   predict various global environmental changes and the impact they may have in the future on the occupation of Canadians in various sectors of the economy

GLOBAL ENVIRONMENTAL CHANGES

Scientists have discovered that Earth goes through periods of warming and cooling over time. They have also found that Earth's mean temperature is directly linked to the amount of carbon (as CO_2) in the atmosphere—increased carbon means increased temperatures. Carbon dioxide, a greenhouse gas, absorbs heat and spreads it through the atmosphere. This greenhouse effect is important because it keeps the planet warm enough for life to exist.

However, human activity has dramatically increased the amounts of carbon dioxide and other greenhouse gases in the atmosphere. Industrialization, the invention of the automobile, and other technologies have contributed greatly to this increase. Over the past few decades, Earth's mean temperature has risen noticeably, and a change of even a single degree can have widespread consequences:

• Melting at the polar icecaps, which causes sea levels to rise

• Increased desertification (conversion of once-arable land to desert conditions)

• More extreme weather events: heat waves, hurricanes, and so forth

• Thawing of the permafrost, which can release methane into the atmosphere

• Endangerment or extinction of certain plants and animals

• Disruption of animal habitats; forced migration

• Spread of tropical diseases (e.g., malaria)

GLOBAL WARMING IN CANADA

Effect on Primary Industries

Primary industries are those that directly gather or otherwise work with raw natural resources: agriculture, forestry, fishing, and so forth. As global warming takes hold, the location and availability of these resources will change. Large areas of Alberta, Saskatchewan, Manitoba, and Ontario will no longer be able to support healthy forests, forcing forestry operations to move further and further north. Those fishing in British Columbia will no longer be able to catch sockeye salmon; the fish will have moved north to Alaska and the Aleutian archipelago. Farmers and ranchers in the southern portions of the prairie provinces may find that conditions are too dry to support crops or livestock.

Effect on Secondary Industries

Secondary industries are those that take raw resources and use them to manufacture goods. The most immediate effects of global warming on secondary industries will be political, legal, and economic. Manufacturing companies will come under ever-increasing pressure to limit the amount of pollution they produce. This will be particularly significant in the automotive and transportation industries since automobiles are major greenhouse gas producers. It also will be more difficult and expensive for companies to obtain the resources they need.

Effect on Tertiary and Quaternary Industries

Tertiary industries include a broad range of service-related jobs: doctors, teachers, telemarketers, politicians, mechanics, and so forth. Jobs in quaternary industries are information-based: research scientists, demographers, and so forth. Because of the wide variety of occupations in these categories, it is difficult to predict what effect global warming will have on them. Any occupation that supports a primary or secondary industry will be affected by changes to those industries; this may mean the loss or relocation of jobs, changes to educational requirements for jobs, or even the creation of jobs related to understanding and preparing for climate change.

PRACTICE QUESTIONS—UNDERSTANDING AND MANAGING CHANGE

1. Approximately what percentage of Toronto's population consists of visible minorities?
   A. 25%
   B. 33%
   C. 50%
   D. 66%

2. Which of the following statements **best** describes cultural assimilation?
   A. Soliciting immigrants from a particular country
   B. Forbidding immigrants from coming to a country
   C. Encouraging immigrants to keep the culture of their old country
   D. Encouraging immigrants to adopt the culture of their new country

3. Multiculturalism is a policy that
   A. promotes cultural separation
   B. promotes cultural superiority
   C. encourages cultural diversity
   D. encourages cultural uniformity

4. Canada's official cultural policy is
   A. colonialism
   B. assimilation
   C. multiculturalism
   D. xenophobic nationalism

5. In which place does Canada rank in terms of the world's largest oil reserves?
   A. Second
   B. Third
   C. Fourth
   D. Fifth

6. Which of the following industries has benefited **most** from the oil sands boom?

    A. Forestry

    B. Agriculture

    C. Construction

    D. Manufacturing

7. The Kyoto Protocol is an international agreement aimed at reducing

    A. deforestation

    B. water pollution

    C. destruction of wetlands

    D. greenhouse gas emissions

8. The government of which of the following provinces is **most** critical of Alberta's oil sands development?

    A. Ontario

    B. Quebec

    C. Saskatchewan

    D. British Columbia

9. Aboriginal people who live near the oil sands are concerned **most** because the oil companies are

    A. not hiring them

    B. polluting their water sources

    C. disrupting their traditional practices

    D. not compensating them for use of their land

10. What is the unofficial capital of the oil sands region?

    A. Edmonton

    B. Cold Lake

    C. Medicine Hat

    D. Fort McMurray

ANSWERS AND SOLUTIONS—PRACTICE QUESTIONS

1. C	3. C	5. A	7. D	9. C
2. D	4. C	6. C	8. A	10. D

1. C

Almost 50% of Toronto's population consists of visible minorities, making it one of the most diverse cities in the world.

2. D

Nations that practise cultural assimilation often are referred to as melting pots; immigrants from all over the world gradually come to adopt a single, uniform culture. Soliciting immigrants from a particular country is usually a colonial practice of encouraging people from the mother country to move to the colony. Forbidding immigration is a hallmark of xenophobia (fear and hatred of foreign influences). Multicultural societies encourage immigrants to keep their culture.

3. C

Multicultural societies are also called cultural mosaics; the national cultural identity is the sum of its various parts. Policies of separation are segregationist and are usually practised in societies that encourage racial discrimination. Policies that promote cultural superiority are signs of extreme nationalism (belief in the superiority of one's nation above all others) and often accompany segregationist policies. Policies that encourage cultural uniformity are assimilation policies.

4. C

Multiculturalism, or cultural diversity, is encouraged and protected by law in Canada. Though once a colony of Great Britain, Canada no longer follows colonialist practices. Canada is not xenophobic; in general, Canadians are receptive to foreign influences. Assimilation is a policy of cultural uniformity and is not practised in Canada.

5. A

The only country with larger oil reserves is Saudi Arabia. Most of Canada's oil reserves are in Alberta's oil sands.

6. C

Because of various infrastructure needs caused by the boom, the construction industry in Alberta is thriving. The other industries are receiving less investment and are experiencing labour shortages as a result of the boom.

7. D

The Kyoto Protocol, often referred to as the Kyoto Accord, commits nations to reducing their greenhouse gas emissions. Canada is one of 183 nations that have ratified the protocol.

8. A

The Ontario government believes that the rapid development of the oil sands has damaged its key industries and is ultimately harmful to Canada's overall economy.

9. C

The activities of the oil companies have affected the local ecosystem, lessening the availability of game and fish. This means that Aboriginal people who practise traditional methods of food-gathering may not be able to sustain themselves. First Nations communities have benefited from employment and compensation, and, to date, there has been no reported contamination of water sources.

10. D

Fort McMurray has grown so rapidly that its infrastructure is under incredible strain; its population more than doubled between 1996 and 2006.

UNIT TEST—UNDERSTANDING AND MANAGING CHANGE

1. What federal department is **primarily** responsible for demography in Canada?

   A. Statistics Canada

   B. Federal Statistics

   C. Dominion Bureau of Statistics

   D. Canadian Demography Department

2. How often is the census conducted in Canada?

   A. Once a year

   B. Once every two years

   C. Once every five years

   D. Once every ten years

3. Which of the following statements describes how the census is conducted in Canada?

   A. Citizens fill out detailed surveys.

   B. Census agents telephone citizens.

   C. Data is acquired from municipal governments.

   D. Data is acquired from provincial governments.

4. The natural increase rate is determined by looking at

   A. birth rate only

   B. immigration rate only

   C. birth rate minus death rate

   D. immigration rate minus emigration rate

5. What two factors does a population pyramid display?

   A. Age and gender

   B. Birth rate and death rate

   C. Immigration rate and emigration rate

   D. Average income and average expenditure

6. Refugees are people who have left their home countries because they

   A. are in danger

   B. cannot make a living

   C. oppose their government

   D. are rejoining their families

7. Economic immigration in Canada comprises approximately what percentage of total immigration?

A. 20%

B. 40%

C. 60%

D. 80%

8. Which of the following factors is **not** a major Canadian pull factor?

A. Culture

B. Climate

C. Economy

D. Government

9. Which of the following two provinces have experienced the **most** growth from internal migration?

A. Ontario and Quebec

B. Saskatchewan and Manitoba

C. British Columbia and Alberta

D. New Brunswick and Nova Scotia

10. Urban sprawl refers to an increase in a city's

A. area

B. density

C. population

D. environmental impact

11. Which of the following policies is the **most viable** solution to urban sprawl?

A. Annexing suburbs

B. Implementing mass transit

C. Increasing residential density

D. Forbidding outward expansion

12. Approximately what percentage of Canada's land is arable?

A. 7%

B. 14%

C. 21%

D. 28%

13. Pesticides are chemicals that
    A. fertilize crops
    B. kill insects and weeds
    C. restore nutrients to soil
    D. eliminate harmful bacteria

14. Which of the following negative consequences does **not** result from soil erosion?
    A. Loss of fertile topsoil
    B. Contamination of groundwater
    C. Contamination of nearby waterways
    D. Increased sedimentation in nearby waterways

15. From which of the following countries does Canada import **most** of its bananas?
    A. Mexico
    B. Ecuador
    C. Honduras
    D. United States

16. Banana production in Latin America is frequently characterized by
    A. violent union activity
    B. human rights violations
    C. United Nations' embargoes
    D. nationalization of plantations

17. Which of the following groups has not pressured banana producers to improve their practices?
    A. Consumers
    B. Supermarkets
    C. The United Nations
    D. Non-governmental organizations

18. The SA8000 is a set of standards regarding
    A. safe agriculture
    B. social accountability
    C. statistical aggregates
    D. sustainable agriculture

ANSWERS AND SOLUTIONS—UNIT TEST

1. A	7. C	13. B
2. C	8. B	14. B
3. A	9. C	15. D
4. C	10. A	16. B
5. A	11. C	17. B
6. A	12. A	18. B

1. A

Statistics Canada, often called StatsCan, is Canada's official demographic organization. It replaced the Dominion Bureau of Statistics in 1971.

2. C

Statistics Canada conducts the census every five years. The next census will take place in 2011.

3. A

Every five years, Canadians must fill out a detailed census form. Canadians can complete this form manually or over the Internet. The last census, and the first to be made available on the Internet, was conducted in 2006.

4. C

Natural increase is determined by subtracting the death rate from the birth rate. Natural increase is an indicator of a country's development: the more developed a nation, the lower its natural increase rate tends to be.

5. A

In a population pyramid, the population of an area is categorized by gender and then ranked by age. For most countries, this type of graph has a generally pyramidal shape.

6. A

Refugees must leave their home country because they are in immediate danger of death, torture, unjust imprisonment, or other such harm. Immigration by people seeking to make a living is economic immigration. Opposition to the government is a push factor. Immigration by people seeking to rejoin their families is family immigration.

7. C

Around 60% of Canada's total immigration is economic immigration. Family immigration accounts for 24%, and refugees account for around 14%.

8. B

A pull factor is something that encourages a prospective immigrant to come to a country. Canada is widely assumed to be characterized by cold temperatures and lots of snow, so our climate is not a major pull factor. Our tolerant culture, strong economy, and stable, democratic government are all strong pull factors.

9. C

British Columbia and Alberta both have thriving primary (resource-based) industries, readily available employment, and strong economies. Therefore, these provinces are attractive destinations for job-seekers, especially skilled tradespersons.

10. A

Urban sprawl is the outward expansion of a city, either directly or through the creation of suburban areas. This outward expansion is not necessarily linked to increasing population; many people simply choose to live in suburban areas and avoid some of the negatives associated with urban living.

11. C

By increasing residential density—zoning high-capacity residential buildings, such as apartments or high-rise condominiums—city governments can lessen the pressure to expand outwards. Annexing suburbs does nothing to combat urban sprawl; implementing mass transit lessens the environmental impact from urban sprawl. Forbidding outward expansion is impractical, at best.

12. A

While 7% may not seem like a lot, Canada's area is so large that 7% is a great amount of arable land.

13. B

To ensure a healthy crop, farmers must eliminate harmful insects and weeds. Pesticides are chemical agents designed to kill unwanted insects and weeds without harming the crops.

14. B

Soil erosion does not directly impact groundwater.

15. D

Although most bananas sold in Canada are grown in Latin America, they enter Canada from the United States as re-exports.

16. B

Child labour, hazardous working conditions, and a variety of other human rights abuses still occur in some plantations today. Unions in Latin America, where they exist at all, tend to be fragmented and largely powerless. The United Nations, particularly the International Labour Organization, has pressured Latin American banana producers to adhere to international human rights laws but has not embargoed any nations. Although some countries, such as Guatemala, have nationalized their banana plantations, the bulk of the banana trade is still carried out by large multinational corporations.

17. B

Supermarkets want to provide customers with low-priced bananas. Because bananas are so popular, customers tend to shop at supermarkets where banana prices are low. The only way for banana producers to keep prices low is to reduce the amount that they spend on such things as wages, safety inspections, and environmental protection.

18. B

The SA8000 was developed by Social Accountability International and is based on the United Nation's Universal Declaration of Human Rights and the conventions of the International Labour Organization.

NOTES

Methods of Historical Inquiry and Communication

METHODS OF HISTORICAL INQUIRY AND COMMUNICATION

This section of the **KEY** can be used throughout the year and with any concept you are learning in class. Methods of historical inquiry and communication provide you with strategies to determine validity in information to help you understand a topic or event, analyze issues and problems from the past, placing people and events in context of time and place, and reflect on perspectives and opinions based on information you have gathered and researched.

5.1.4   organize and record information gathered through research

RESEARCH

When you are asked to research a topic, you need to find ideas and information related to it. These ideas and information will be basic to the substance, or main body, of your research. Following through with some or all of the steps and strategies below will help you keep your research manageable, find reliable resources, and acknowledge the experts and authors who provided you with your information.

CREATE A RESEARCH PLAN

A checklist-style plan can help you stay focused and on track, as shown in the following example:

1. Topic chosen: _____

2. Assignment expectations: _____

3. KWL chart created

4. Webbing for preliminary ideas

Example

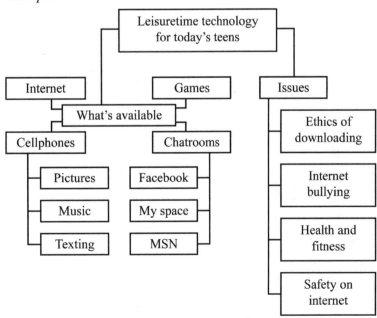

5. Topic restated as a question

6. Preview of available information in the form of a quick list of readily available resources, people you could interview, etc.

7. Preliminary research conclusion—does my topic need to be adjusted so that it fits available resources?

8. Further questions related to the topic _____

9. Data collected and point-form notes completed

10. Source information recorded for bibliography

11. Information organized and outline drafted

12. Rough draft of paper completed

13. Good copy of paper completed

14. Bibliography added

15. Title page and table of contents added

Sticking to these steps will ensure that your writing will be the best that it can be on the day the assignment is due.

RECORD INFORMATION

As long as you record your information and research, any method you use is fine. One possible method you could use to record your information and research is to organize it in point form. You could use index cards to record your information, with perhaps one source per index card. Keeping your information organized helps you to

- access the information later

- ensure that you never plagiarize

- keep quotes and sources of quotes separate from your other information

Make simple headings on index cards to organize your information, using practical topic headings, such as "Quotations" or "References," so that you have a written record of your information. Computers, lined paper, or index cards are all good places to keep track of your sources.

5.1.3   evaluate the credibility of sources and information

CHECKING RELIABILITY

How do you decide whether or not to believe what you read? Can you tell fact from opinion? How do you decide whether or not you can trust the author?

Factual statements are clear, accurate, and verifiable. Much of what you read has not been tested, but you usually accept it because it appears to be true or others whom you trust say that it is true. Magazines, books, newspapers, websites, bulletin boards, and blogs, for example, should not be trusted until the authors' knowledge and experience on the subject has been verified. Faulty conclusions are often made because the evidence that is relied on may be based either on incorrect observations or observations that are prejudiced, wishful, or imaginative.

In order to determine how credible a piece of writing is, try examining it from the following angles:

Author's viewpoint: Who is the author? What does he or she stand to gain or lose? An article about politics may be very biased if it is written, for example, by the leader of a political party.

Text structure: Is the information well presented? Are the arguments easy to understand, logical, and supported by reasonable evidence? Sloppy work may indicate that the work is not credible.

Author's word choice: Do the author's words express ideas and convey facts, or are they meant to inflame readers' emotions? Does the author's tone seem balanced or angry?

FINAL TIPS ON RELIABILITY AND ACCURACY

- Compare facts using various resources, and watch for differences and contradictions.

- Consider the publishing date: is the information current?

- Consider the expertise and reputation of the source.

- Watch for biases. Is the information objective, or does it favour/criticize a particular group?

- Double-check Internet sources: is there proof of the author's expertise? Is the site reliable overall? How recent is the information on the website? Is the website educational or commercial in nature?

- Double-checking accuracy is an important part of publishing your work. Make sure your information is valid before doing a final print of your assignment.

5.1.2   select and use a wide variety of relevant primary and secondary sources that represent a diverse range of perspectives

PRIMARY AND SECONDARY SOURCES

Primary and secondary sources can sometimes determine the degree of accuracy and reliability of the information. Research articles with a variety of sources can usually be taken more seriously than a research article that does not use many sources.

Primary and secondary sources are both important elements of research. The following chart shows examples of both kinds of sources.

Primary Source	Secondary Source
Autobiography	Biography
Interview with a Titanic survivor	News story written after the Titanic sank
Original manuscript of a book	Translated or revised edition of a book

Interviews can be either primary or secondary sources of information. For example, if you were doing a research paper on the Quebec ice storm, a primary source interview would be with a person who lived through the disaster. A secondary source interview would be with a professor who studies the impact of disasters on regions in Canada. Both primary and secondary source interviews are excellent sources for gathering information you might not find in a book.

SEARCHING

You can search at your library to find materials that are related to your topic by typing in any piece of information from the following list:

- title

- keyword

- author

- subject

- call number

- series title

- ISBN/ISSN: This is a cataloguing number found at the bottom of the credits page, and it looks like this: 0-03-052664-7 5-048 04 03 02 (These numbers represent a text entitled *Elements of Language: A Second Course*)

Your catalogue search could produce titles and call numbers for several books on your topic, and you can take that information with you to your local library.

AT THE LIBRARY

When you go to a library, the librarian can help you find the information you are looking for. Most libraries are divided into sections to help people easily locate materials. Some sections that the librarian might show you include:

- reference materials (dictionaries, encyclopedias, atlases). Usually, these books may only be used in

- the library

- audio/visual (movies, music, games)

- periodicals (newspapers, magazines, journals)

- non-fiction books

All library books are classified or grouped according to one of two systems: the Dewey Decimal System or the Library of Congress Classification (LCC). Most Canadian and American libraries use the Dewey Decimal System. Usually, only very large libraries use the Library of Congress Classification. The following tables show how these two systems organize non-fiction books by number or letter.

Dewey Decimal System	
000	General works
100	Philosophy
200	Religion
300	Social sciences
400	Language
500	Science
600	Technology
700	Fine arts
800	Literature
900	History and geography

Library of Congress System	
A	General works
B	Philosophy, psychology, religion
C	History and related sciences
D	History: general and Old World
E–F	History: the Americas
G	Geography, anthropology, recreation
H	Social sciences
J	Political science
K	Law
L	Education
M	Music
N	Fine arts
P	Language and literature
Q	Science
R	Medicine
S	Agriculture
T	Technology
U	Military science
V	Naval science
Z	Bibliography and library science

The following chart explains the Dewey Decimal System classification for a book called *The Biology of the Honey Bee*, by Mark L. Winston.

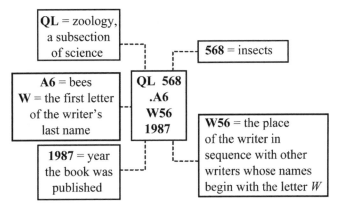

To find this book in the library, look in numerical order in the QL section for 568. Then, look in alphabetical order in the books under QL568 for A6. Finally, look at the books under QL568.A6 for W56.

ONLINE SEARCHES

Online searches involve using keywords and phrases related to your topic. Be as specific as possible when searching. For example, the keywords "Provincial election in Ontario" will yield more specific results than just using the keywords "Provincial election." Sometimes, you have to try a few different keywords or phrases before you find sites that match what you are trying to research. When you find an article related to your topic, watch for hyperlinks to other related articles or websites.

The sites that are listed first in an online search are determined differently depending on which search engine you are using. Some search engines index sites by number of hits or by number of links to a site. Sometimes, the owners of websites will pay to be ranked on the first page of a search. Usually, the websites listed on the first page of your search results will be the most relevant, but this is not always the case. Play around with keywords and phrases. Often, if you see the same sites more than once, those sites are likely to be relevant.

Information from the Internet is like any other kind of published information, so you must make sure to cite the information in your bibliography if you use any material from an online source.

DICTIONARIES AND ENCYCLOPEDIAS

Dictionaries and encyclopedias are among the most useful reference materials in the library. Both dictionaries and encyclopedias can be particularly useful when you are starting a research project and want basic information.

Dictionaries are a good place to start when you are looking for the meaning of a word. Look for the meaning of the word associated with the specific subject or content area. For instance, the word revolution, shown in the sample dictionary definition below, is used in both science and social studies, but the word has two totally different meanings.

> **rev•o•lu•tion** (rev′ə lōō′shən), n. **1.** the overthrow and replacement of an established government or political system by the people governed. **2.** a sudden, complete, or radical change. **3.** rotation on or as if on an axis. **4.** the orbiting of one celestial body around another. **5.** a single cycle in a rotation or orbit. **–rev′o•lu′•tion•ary′**, *adj., n., pl* **–ies. –rev′o•lu′•tion•ist**, n.

Encyclopedias are reliable sources of basic information about a variety of topics. Most libraries do not allow you to take encyclopedias out of the library, so you will have to do your research in the library. Remember that libraries also have electronic encyclopedias on CD-ROMs. The advantage of electronic encyclopedias is that the information is regularly updated as needed. If you want to cite a CD-ROM for a research paper, the following example shows a citation of a CD-ROM as it would appear in a bibliography.

> "Title of Article." Title of Database. Medium (CD-ROM). Electronic Publisher, publication date.

Example

> "Technology." Encyclopaedia Britannica. CD-ROM. Encyclopaedia Britannica, Inc., 2008.

CD-ROMs on many subjects and topics are available through your library. You can reference them in the same way as a CD-ROM encyclopedia. You can also access all major encyclopedias, such as Encyclopaedia Britannia Online, from your computer. This is much cheaper than purchasing a printed set of encyclopedias.

INTERVIEWING EXPERTS

Interviews with experts or community members can also yield excellent information. Interviews are especially useful if you are reporting on something that is very current. Chances are there will not be much information on a very new topic or event going on in your area. In this situation, an interview might be the best resource for getting up-to-date information.

5.3.2   use an accepted form of documentation to acknowledge all sources of information, including electronic sources

DOCUMENTATION

BIBLIOGRAPHIES

In order to create a complete and correct bibliography, you will need to record a variety of information for all sources used in your research, including author, title, publisher, website information, place of publication, and volume number.

Always follow the guidelines for creating a bibliography laid out by your teacher. The following formats provide examples of how you could record source information for references used in your research.

Book

Author. *Title*. City: Publisher, Year.

Example

McCrae, Andrew. *Teens and Their Culture*.

Boston: Boston University Press, 2006.

Periodical (magazine, newspaper)

Author. "Title of Article." *Publication Name*, Date.

Example

Brolin, Megan. "Online Predators." *Teen by Teen News*, May 7, 2007.

Encyclopedia

"Name of Article." *Title of Book*, Edition number. Publisher, Date.

Example

"Technology." *Encyclopaedia Britannica*, 15th ed. Encyclopaedia Britannica, Inc., 2007.

Electronic Sources

Author (if known). "Document Title." Website or Database Title. Date of electronic publication. Name of Sponsoring Institution. Date information was accessed. <URL>

"Internet Safety Network for Teens." Parent Share. July 2006. Ontario Association of Children's Aid Societies. Nov 2007. <http://www.occas.org/childwelfare/links.htm>

INFORMATION SOURCES

You can access online library catalogues by typing the name of your local library into an Internet search (for example, Toronto Public Library, Burlington Public Library, Thunder Bay Public Library, etc.). When you perform this search, you will find links to

- library catalogues

- databases by subject or title or frequently asked questions, such as "How do I use the library catalogue?"

5.1.1   formulate questions for researching and inquiry and develop a plan to guide research

FORMULATING QUESTIONS

QUESTIONS TO GUIDE YOUR INQUIRY

Once you have chosen a topic, try to think of some questions that will help you to focus or direct your inquiry. For instance, if you chose the topic "The Element of Surprise at Pearl Harbor," you might ask the following questions:

- How exactly did the Japanese launch a surprise attack on Pearl Harbor?

- Where in Pearl Harbor did they attack?

- How did the Americans respond to the attack?

- What did the Americans learn from this event?

- Did the Japanese successfully complete any other surprise attacks during World War II? If so, where?

- How did the Americans use the element of surprise to turn the tables on the Japanese?

To keep your research focused and effective, you need to evaluate your questions. You may choose to eliminate some questions that are not relevant enough to your topic, such as the last two questions on the list above.

You may wish to arrange the questions in a logical order to help you to organize the information for your paper. Often, key questions can be used as sub-topics for your paper. For example, if the main topic for your paper is "Where in Pearl Harbor did the Japanese attack?" a subheading for your paper could be "Attack Targets."

IDENTIFYING KEYWORDS AND PHRASES

The topic and inquiry questions you have generated can provide a great starting point for your research. As you begin to find books and Internet articles on your topic, watch for keywords and phrases that you can use to find more in-depth information. Some keywords and phrases that would help you with Pearl Harbor research, for example, might include:

- Hickam Air Force Base

- Bellows Air Force Station

- Wheeler Army Airfield

- Casualties at Pearl Harbor

- United States Intelligence, Pearl Harbor

- Surprise attack on Pearl Harbor

- Aftermath of Pearl Harbor

- Warnings before the attack on Pearl Harbor

Staying organized about keywords and phrases will ensure that you do not forget any part of your assignment that you want to include. There are many different methods to get you started in developing the content of your work; try a variety of methods to see which work the best for you.

Organizing your information will help you at several stages in the writing process. Staying organized while you are forming ideas at the developing stage of a writing assignment helps you understand what you want to write about. It also gives you ideas of the information you can use in your assignment. You can keep tabs on what information you want to use and what you might eventually like to leave out.

Once your ideas are developed, organizing your information helps your reader understand your ideas more precisely. Being organized in your writing helps you create clearly formed ideas and helps you get those ideas across to your reader. Use the methods that work the best for you. Time spent organizing before you sit down to write will save you a lot of time in the long run and will ensure that you create the best writing possible.

5.2.5   *draw conclusions based on supporting evidence, effective analysis of information, and awareness of diverse historical interpretations*

DRAWING CONCLUSIONS

FACT AND OPINION

Facts are statements that can be proven true. You can use experiments, research, or observations to prove facts. Opinions are statements that express personal beliefs. Opinions cannot always be proven. Sometimes, it is difficult to tell the difference between fact and opinion, and other times, it is very obvious. As the reader, you must try to separate the two. Almanacs, encyclopedias, and atlases are examples of books that are usually reliable sources of factual information.

Factual statements are ones that can be proven to be true. Much of what people read is not necessarily verified, but readers usually accept it because it appears to be true or others say the information is true. Magazines, books, newspapers, the Internet, websites, bulletin boards, and blogs, for example, should not be entirely trusted until the knowledge and experience of the author has been verified.

People often also reach faulty conclusions because the evidence they use may be based on either faulty observations or observations that may be prejudiced, wishful, or imaginative.

Not everything that is stated with authority is really fact. Generally, people tend to think that information in encyclopedias is fact. There are many other resources, such as eyewitness accounts, newspaper accounts, supermarket tabloid accounts, and the Internet, that are often less reliable than reference materials you can find at the library. Information on the Internet often has errors or is biased.

How do you determine what makes a resource reliable as a source of information? When is the information valid and authentic? What kinds of sources will mostly provide accurate information?

It is important to be critical of what you read, particularly when the information you are reading claims to be factual or truthful. Evaluate the stated facts carefully. Decide what evidence is convincing and what might need verification. Look for biases that suggest a particular viewpoint or opinion, even when the bias is not directly stated. If a newspaper, for example, reports mostly stories and articles that cast a particular politician or political party in a negative light, you could probably draw the conclusion that the paper does not support the policies of that politician or her party. It is a good idea to not read a newspaper that has a bias, or to balance your knowledge of issues by reading a variety of news sources.

5.2.1   analyse information, employing concepts and theories appropriate to historical inquiry

ANALYSING INFORMATION

LOCATING AND RECALLING INFORMATION

As you read, you need to remember the events of a story or an article in order to understand them. Events can be structured in terms of idea and example, cause and effect, or chronological sequence. You will find that you often use combinations of these concepts.

Idea and Example

An idea-and-example structure is one in which an idea is presented and then followed by specific evidence, as shown in the following paragraph from "Poisonous Spiders."

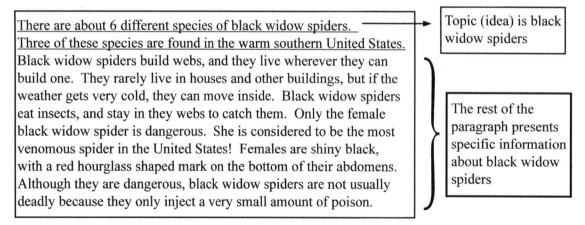

There are about 6 different species of black widow spiders. Three of these species are found in the warm southern United States. Black widow spiders build webs, and they live wherever they can build one. They rarely live in houses and other buildings, but if the weather gets very cold, they can move inside. Black widow spiders eat insects, and stay in they webs to catch them. Only the female black widow spider is dangerous. She is considered to be the most venomous spider in the United States! Females are shiny black, with a red hourglass shaped mark on the bottom of their abdomens. Although they are dangerous, black widow spiders are not usually deadly because they only inject a very small amount of poison.

Topic (idea) is black widow spiders

The rest of the paragraph presents specific information about black widow spiders

Cause and Effect

Authors use cause and effect to develop a paragraph. These paragraphs explain why events happened and why things are as they are. Cause and effect is often used in writing that informs, explains, or persuades. Some cause-and-effect words are because, as a result, why, when, therefore, so, for this reason, and if … then. A cause-and-effect structure shows how one event determines a specific outcome. In the following passage, look at how a cause-and-effect structure is used to describe how the bubonic plague spread.

THE BLACK DEATH: BUBONIC PLAGUE

In the early 1330s, an outbreak of deadly bubonic plague occurred in China. The bubonic plague mainly affects rodents, but fleas can transmit the disease to people. Once people are infected, they infect others very rapidly. Plague causes fever and a painful swelling of the lymph glands called buboes, which is how it gets its name. The disease also causes spots on the skin that are red at first and then turn black.

Since China was one of the busiest of the world's trading nations, it was only a matter of time before the outbreak of plague in China spread to western Asia and Europe. In October of 1347, several Italian merchant ships returned from a trip to the Black Sea, one of the key links in trade with China. When the ships docked in Sicily, many of those on board were already dying of plague. Within days, the disease spread to the city and the surrounding countryside.

Cause	Effect
Bubonic plague develops in Chinese rodents.	Fleas transfer the disease to people.
Infected people transmit the bubonic plague.	Fever, "buboes" (swollen glands), and spots on the skin are some plague symptoms.
China is a large trading nation.	Plague spreads to western Asia and Europe.
In 1347, ships from China arrive in Sicily.	Disease spreads from the ships' crews and passengers to Sicilians.
The disease spreads quickly all across Europe.	About one-third of Europe's population dies of plague.

Chronological Sequence

The world is primarily ordered by time. Time order affects all aspects of life. If you look for a logical time order (chronology) while reading, you will find it easier to locate and recall information. For example, if you wanted to name the last five premiers of Ontario, you would list them in chronological order, as shown:

David Peterson	1985–1990
Bob Rae	1990–1995
Mike Harris	1995–2002
Ernie Eves	2002–2003
Dalton McGuinty	2003–present

Chronological order refers to what happened or what is happening over a certain time period. Authors organize and present their ideas chronologically when they want to present a series of events or show the order in which steps may occur.

Sometimes, the best way to remember the events of a story is to just think about them in the order in which they occurred. Chronological (or time-order) sequencing is a method for ensuring that events are presented in their proper order or chronology. The article "Black Death: Bubonic Plague" presents its ideas in chronological order, making the sequence of events—included in the table following this article—easy to follow.

THE BLACK DEATH: BUBONIC PLAGUE

In the early 1330s, an outbreak of deadly bubonic plague occurred in China. The bubonic plague mainly affects rodents, but fleas can transmit the disease to people. Once people are infected, they infect others very rapidly. Plague causes fever and a painful swelling of the lymph glands called buboes, which is how it gets its name. The disease also causes spots on the skin that are red at first and then turn black.

Since China was one of the busiest of the world's trading nations, it was only a matter of time before the outbreak of plague in China spread to western Asia and Europe. In October of 1347, several Italian merchant ships returned from a trip to the Black Sea, one of the key links in trade with China. When the ships docked in Sicily, many of those on board were already dying of plague. Within days, the disease spread to the city and the surrounding countryside. An eyewitness tells what happened:

"Realizing what a deadly disaster had come to them, the people quickly drove the Italians from their city. But the disease remained, and soon death was everywhere. Fathers abandoned their sick sons. Lawyers refused to come and make out wills for the dying. Friars and nuns were left to care for the sick, and monasteries and convents were soon deserted, as they were stricken, too. Bodies were left in empty houses, and there was no one to give them a Christian burial."

The disease struck and killed people with terrible speed. The Italian writer Boccaccio said its victims often "ate lunch with their friends and dinner with their ancestors in paradise."

By the following August, the plague had spread as far north as England, where people called it "The Black Death" because of the black spots it produced on the skin. A terrible killer was loose across Europe, and medieval medicine had nothing to combat it.

In winter, the disease seemed to disappear, but only because fleas—which were now helping to carry it from person to person—are dormant then. Each spring, the plague attacked again, killing new victims. After five years, 25 million people were dead—one-third of Europe's people.

Even when the worst was over, smaller outbreaks continued, not just for years, but for centuries. The survivors lived in constant fear of the plague's return, and the disease did not disappear until the 1600s.

Medieval society never recovered from the results of the plague. So many people had died that there were serious labour shortages all over Europe. This led workers to demand higher wages, but landlords refused those demands. By the end of the 1300s, peasant revolt broke out in England, France, Belgium, and Italy.

The disease took its toll on the church as well. People throughout Christendom had prayed devoutly for deliverance from the plague. Why hadn't those prayers been answered? A new period of political turmoil and philosophical questioning lay ahead.

Chronological Sequence	
Year	Event
Early 1330s	Outbreak of bubonic plague in China
1347	Italian ships brought plague to Europe from China
1348	Plague reached England
By 1352	25 million Europeans had died
1352–1600s	Small outbreaks of plague continued
1600s	Plague finally disappeared

5.2.3   analyze historical events and issues from the perspectives of different participants in those events and issues

ASSESSING BOTH SIDES OF AN ISSUE

In order to become a skilled debater on any issue, it is an excellent strategy to be equally well prepared to argue or defend either side of an argument. Exploring both sides of an issue also helps you to understand opinions that may differ from your own. You will become more confident and comfortable with your own viewpoint if you can support it with evidence.

Consider the following graphic organizer, which presents both sides of the controversial issue, "Are zoos moral?" Some people feel strongly opposed to the very idea of animals being held in captivity so that people can watch them for money. Others find zoos to be an acceptable source of entertainment and education. Who is right? After looking at the supporting evidence for both sides, your conclusion may turn out to be somewhat of a compromise of the two opposing viewpoints. This often happens in real arguments and is an ideal approach to respecting different opinions.

Supporting Arguments		Opposing Arguments
Help educate people about different animals in their area		Animals show signs of stress, boredom, and unhappiness
Protect endangered animals		Animals belong in their natural habitats
Provide scientists with a place to study animals up close		Some animals are abused in captivity
Provide veterinarians and zoologists with a place to learn about caring for wild animals	**Should there be zoos?**	Scientists would learn more by studying animals in the wild
Help injured animals that could not survive in the wild		The natural world is for the survival of the fittest; humans should not interfere
Make money that can pay for animal care in the wild		Humans do not have the right to capture animals
Zoos, wildlife preserves, and aquariums may be the only place for some people to see wild animals and learn about them		Animals are forced to entertain. Parks make lots of money that is not all used for animal welfare

Conclusion

Zoos could be created so that the animals can live in conditions similar to their natural habitats with minimal interference from people. Wildlife preserves help protect animals from the expansion of towns and cities. These preserves can provide a safe haven for migrating birds and animals.

Reasons

• The welfare of the animals is important; they do not choose to be in a zoo.

• People sometimes cause problems for animals in the wild by invading their habitats.

• Zoos can help educate people about the importance of protecting wildlife and living in harmony with animals. People should not destroy animals' homes or kill for fun or body parts.

• Videos can be used to show animals in their natural world. Thus people do not have to capture animals and put them on display.

BIASES

Bias is an unconscious or natural tendency to adopt a preferred view on something. It may be unspoken, but is often expressed in attitude or behaviour. It can certainly be positive, as in having an inner pride in being Canadian, which would be a pro-Canada bias, or having a bias to cheer for your home team no matter what. However, there are negative biases, such as

• **anti-youth bias**, which refers to assumptions made about young people, including misconceptions about the trustworthiness of youth.

• **anti-aging bias**, which refers to assumptions made about older people, which can include misconceptions that they are obsolete because of their age.

• **anti-authority bias**, which makes a person view teachers, parents, policemen, or other authority figures with hostility and suspicion.

• **racial prejudice**, which makes a person dislike or hate anyone who looks different from their own ethnic group.

Other biases include political biases, gender biases, economic biases, and religious biases. Negative biases prevent people from being tolerant of other people and different viewpoints.

Key Strategies for Success on Tests

KEY STRATEGIES FOR SUCCESS ON TESTS

THINGS TO CONSIDER WHEN TAKING A TEST

It is normal to feel anxious before you write a test. You can manage this anxiety by using the following strategies:

- Think positive thoughts. Imagine yourself doing well on the test.
- Make a conscious effort to relax by taking several slow, deep, controlled breaths. Concentrate on the air going in and out of your body.
- Before you begin the test, ask questions if you are unsure of anything.
- Jot down key words or phrases from any instructions your teacher gives you.
- Look over the entire test to find out the number and kinds of questions on the test.
- Read each question closely, and reread if necessary.
- Pay close attention to key vocabulary words. Sometimes, these words are **bolded** or *italicized*, and they are usually important words in the question.
- If you are putting your answers on an answer sheet, mark your answers carefully. Always print clearly. If you wish to change an answer, erase the mark completely, and ensure that your final answer is darker than the one you have erased.
- Use highlighting to note directions, key words, and vocabulary that you find confusing or that are important to answering the question.
- Double-check to make sure you have answered everything before handing in your test.
- When taking tests, students often overlook the easy words. Failure to pay close attention to these words can result in an incorrect answer. One way to avoid this is to be aware of these words and to underline, circle, or highlight them while you are taking the test.
- Even though some words are easy to understand, they can change the meaning of the entire question, so it is important that you pay attention to them. Here are some examples.

all	always	most likely	probably	best	not
difference	usually	except	most	unlikely	likely

Example

1. Which of the following expressions is **incorrect**?
    A. $3 + 2 \geq 5$
    B. $4 - 3 < 2$
    C. $5 \times 4 < 15$
    D. $6 \times 3 \geq 18$

TEST PREPARATION AND TEST-TAKING SKILLS

HELPFUL STRATEGIES FOR ANSWERING MULTIPLE-CHOICE QUESTIONS

A multiple-choice question gives you some information and then asks you to select an answer from four choices. Each question has one correct answer. The other choices are distractors, which are incorrect.

The following strategies can help you when answering multiple-choice questions:

- Quickly skim through the entire test. Find out how many questions there are, and plan your time accordingly.

- Read and reread questions carefully. Underline key words, and try to think of an answer before looking at the choices.

- If there is a graphic, look at the graphic, read the question, and go back to the graphic. Then, you may want to underline the important information from the question.

- Carefully read the choices. Read the question first and then each choice that goes with it.

- When choosing an answer, try to eliminate those choices that are clearly wrong or do not make sense.

- Some questions may ask you to select the best answer. These questions will always include words like *best*, *most appropriate*, or *most likely*. All of the choices will be correct to some degree, but one of the choices will be better than the others in some way. Carefully read all four choices before choosing the answer you think is the best.

- If you do not know the answer, or if the question does not make sense to you, it is better to guess than to leave it blank.

- Do not spend too much time on any one question. Make a mark (*) beside a difficult question, and come back to it later. If you are leaving a question to come back to later, make sure you also leave the space on the answer sheet, if you are using one.

- Remember to go back to the difficult questions at the end of the test; sometimes, clues are given throughout the test that will provide you with answers.

- Note any negative words like *no* or *not*, and be sure your answer fits the question.

- Before changing an answer, be sure you have a very good reason to do so.

- Do not look for patterns on your answer sheet, if you are using one.

HELPFUL STRATEGIES FOR ANSWERING WRITTEN-RESPONSE QUESTIONS

A written response requires you to respond to a question or directive indicated by words such as *explain*, *predict*, *list*, *describe*, *show your work*, *solve*, or *calculate*. The following strategies can help you when answering written-response questions:

- Read and reread the question carefully.

- Recognize and pay close attention to directing words such as *explain*, *show your work*, and *describe*.

- Underline key words and phrases that indicate what is required in your answer, such as *explain*, *estimate*, *answer*, *calculate*, or *show your work*.

- Write down rough, point-form notes regarding the information you want to include in your answer.

- Think about what you want to say, and organize information and ideas in a coherent and concise manner within the time limit you have for the question.

- Be sure to answer every part of the question that is asked.

- Include as much information as you can when you are asked to explain your thinking.

- Include a picture or diagram if it will help to explain your thinking.

- Try to put your final answer to a problem in a complete sentence to be sure it is reasonable.

- Reread your response to ensure you have answered the question.

- Ask yourself if your answer makes sense.

- Ask yourself if your answer sounds right.

- Use appropriate subject vocabulary and terms in your response.

TEST PREPARATION COUNTDOWN

If you develop a plan for studying and test preparation, you will perform well on tests.

Here is a general plan to follow seven days before you write a test.

COUNTDOWN: 7 DAYS BEFORE THE TEST

1. Use "Finding Out about the Test" to help you make your own personal test preparation plan.
2. Review the following information:
   - Areas to be included on the test
   - Types of test items
   - General and specific test tips

3. Start preparing for the test at least seven days before the test. Develop your test preparation plan, and set time aside to prepare and study.

COUNTDOWN: 6, 5, 4, 3, 2 DAYS BEFORE THE TEST

1. Review old homework assignments, quizzes, and tests.
2. Rework problems on quizzes and tests to make sure you still know how to solve them.
3. Correct any errors made on quizzes and tests.
4. Review key concepts, processes, formulas, and vocabulary.
5. Create practice test questions for yourself, and answer them. Work out many sample problems.

COUNTDOWN: THE NIGHT BEFORE THE TEST

1. Use the night before the test for final preparation, which includes reviewing and gathering materials needed for the test before going to bed.
2. Most importantly, get a good night's rest, and know you have done everything possible to do well on the test.

TEST DAY

1. Eat a healthy and nutritious breakfast.
2. Ensure you have all the necessary materials.
3. Think positive thoughts, such as "I can do this," "I am ready," and "I know I can do well."
4. Arrive at your school early, so you are not rushing, which can cause you anxiety and stress.

SUMMARY OF HOW TO BE SUCCESSFUL DURING A TEST

You may find some of the following strategies useful for writing a test:

- Take two or three deep breaths to help you relax.

- Read the directions carefully, and underline, circle, or highlight any important words.

- Look over the entire test to understand what you will need to do.

- Budget your time.

- Begin with an easy question or a question you know you can answer correctly rather than follow the numerical question order of the test.

- If you cannot remember how to answer a question, try repeating the deep breathing and physical relaxation activities. Then, move on to visualization and positive self-talk to get yourself going.

- When answering questions with graphics (pictures, diagrams, tables, or graphs), look at the question carefully, and use the following steps:

  1. Read the title of the graphic and any key words.

  2. Read the test question carefully to figure out what information you need to find in the graphic.

  3. Go back to the graphic to find the information you need.

- Write down anything you remember about the subject on the reverse side of your test paper. This activity sometimes helps to remind you that you do know something and are capable of writing the test.

- Look over your test when you have finished, and double-check your answers to be sure you did not forget anything.

Practice Test

PRACTICE TEST

Table of Correlations	
Specific Expectation	**Practice Test**
Students are expected to:	
1.1 **describe the components and patterns of Canada's spatial organization**	
1.1.1 explain the terms and concepts associated with regions	23
1.1.2 describe the characteristics of natural systems	24, 25
1.1.3 describe the characteristics of human systems	26
1.1.4 outline the criteria used to define selected Canadian ecozones and describe the processes and interactions that shape those coziness	27
1.1.5 distinguish between the characteristics of urban and rural environments	28
1.1.6 explain the geographical requirements that determine the location of businesses, industries, and transportation systems	29
1.2 **demonstrate an understanding of the regional diversity of Canada's natural and human systems**	
1.2.1 analyse variations in population density and use their findings to explain overall population patterns	30
1.2.2 illustrate and explain the regional distribution patterns of various peoples across Canada	31
1.2.3 analyse the location pattern of recent First Nation land claims in Canada	32
1.3 **analyse local and regional factors that affect Canada's natural and human systems**	
1.3.1 identify criteria with which to evaluate the effect of government land use policy on planning in the local community	33
1.3.2 compare different ways of providing human systems for a territory and areas in southern Canada	34
1.3.3 use a reasoned argument to identify the best place to live in Canada and justify their choice	35
1.3.4 predict future locations of businesses, industries, and transportation systems in Canada	36
1.3.5 identify and describe examples of Canadian art that reflect natural or cultural landscapes	37
2.1 **explain the relationship of Canada's renewable and non-renewable resources to the Canadian economy**	
2.1.1 explain how human activities affect, or are affected by, the environment	38, 39
2.1.2 describe how natural systems influence cultural and economic activities	40
2.1.3 describe the regional distribution of Canada's energy sources and the relative importance of each source	41
2.1.4 identify the role of government in managing resources and protecting the environment	42
2.1.5 explain the ways in which the traditional ecological knowledge of Aboriginal peoples, including their concepts of place, wilderness, and boundaries, influences how they interact with their environment	43
2.2 **analyse the ways in which natural systems interact with human systems and make predictions about the outcomes of these interactions**	
2.2.1 assess the value of Canada's key natural resources, including agricultural lands and wilderness	44, 45
2.2.2 assess the feasibility of using selected renewable and alternative energy sources to implement conservation strategies	46
2.2.3 evaluate differing viewpoints on the benefits and disadvantages of selected resource megaprojects	47

2.2.4	assess how the effect of urban growth alters the natural environment	48
2.2.5	present findings from research on ways of improving the balance between human and natural systems	49
2.3	**evaluate various ways of ensuring resource sustainability in Canada**	
2.3.1	analyse and evaluate the success, in environmental and economic terms, of local waste management methods	50
2.3.2	evaluate solutions to environmental problems proposed by various groups and make recommendations for sustainable resources use	51
2.3.3	recommend ways in which individuals can contribute to the quality of life in their home, local econzone, province, nation, and the world	52
3.1	**describe how Canada's diverse geography affects its economic, cultural, and environmental links to other countries**	
3.1.1	explain the role of selected international organizations and agreements and why Canada participates in them	1, 2
3.1.2	summarize significant contributions Canada makes to the world	3
3.1.3	explain how Canada's natural systems form part of global natural systems	4, 5
3.2	**analyse connections between Canada and other countries**	
3.2.1	compare Canada's approaches to specific concerns with the approaches of other nations	6, 7
3.2.2	evaluate Canada's participation in organizations that deal with global issues	8
3.2.3	analyse the global distribution of selected commodities and determine Canada's share of each	9
3.2.4	summarize ways in which the economies of Canada and the rest of the world are interdependent	10, 11
3.2.5	evaluate the importance of tourism to Canada's economic development	12, 13
3.3	**report on global issues that affect Canadians**	
3.3.1	compare, in terms of resource use and consumption, the "ecological footprint" of an average Canadian with that of an average citizen in a developing country	14
3.3.2	produce a set of guidelines for developing a solution to a global geographic or environmental issue	15
4.1	**explain how natural and human systems change over time and from place to place**	
4.1.2	explain how selected factors cause change in human and natural systems	18, 21
4.2	**predict how current or anticipated changes in the geography of Canada will affect the country's future economic, social, and environmental well-being**	
4.2.2	predict the consequences of human activities on natural systems	22
4.2.3	analyse the positive and negative effects on people and the environment of the manufacturer, transportation to market, and consumption of selected products	16, 17, 19
4.3	**explain how global economic and environmental factors affect individual choices**	
4.3.1	evaluate the impact of change on a selected planning project	20

PRACTICE TEST

1. The United Nations is known for all of the following initiatives **except**

   A. supporting human rights

   B. developing guidelines for international trade

   C. assisting countries following natural disasters

   D. protecting the sustainability of the environment

2. Participation in which of the following international organizations fosters Canada's **greatest** opportunity to gain overseas trading partners?

   A. NAFTA

   B. United Nations

   C. World Trade Organization

   D. Asia-Pacific Economic Cooperation

3. The Canadian International Development Agency (CIDA) was formed to help people in regions of the world who encounter difficult circumstances. Which of the following circumstances would CIDA not help with?

   A. Famine

   B. Natural disasters

   C. Depletion of natural resources

   D. Atmospheric cleansing of energy emissions

4. The location of Earth's __*i*__ is strongly related to where particular __*ii*__ exist in the world. The given statement is correctly completed by the information in which of the following rows?

Row	*i*	*ii*
A.	global biomes	climate patterns
B.	ecosystems	tectonic plates
C.	crustal plates	human systems
D.	Ring of Fire	global biomes

5. Which of the following factors is **not** a major contributor to the formation of Earth's global climate system?

   A. Influence of the atmosphere

   B. Circulation of ocean waters

   C. Location of the continents

   D. Differences in landforms

6. Which of the following statements **best** explains a concern of some environmentalists toward 20-year forestry plans?

   A. They feel the time period should be 30 years so that natural systems can become re-established and various forestry operations can be completed.

   B. They feel the time period should be 10 years so that any new and environmentally friendly technologies in forestry can be used.

   C. They feel the time period should be 5 years because the political party in power can change during 20 years.

   D. They feel that forestry plans should be rewritten every year so that plans are kept up to date.

7. Government measures to ensure the responsible use of Canada's resources would benefit all of the following concerns **except**

   A. freezing rain

   B. pesticide use

   C. deforestation

   D. cross-border pollution

8. Which of the following issues would **least likely** be addressed by organizations that deal with global issues?

   A. Human rights

   B. Deforestation

   C. Global warming

   D. Decline of fish stocks

Use the following information to answer the next question.

> Canada has the second-largest oil reserves in the world.

9. For which of the following reasons does Canada **most likely** import oil from other countries?

   A. Canada requires a higher grade of oil in some industries.

   B. Canada does not have adequate economic funds to produce oil.

   C. It costs too much to get oil out of Alberta's large oilsands projects.

   D. It costs less to import oil in some places in Canada than it does to transport it nationally.

10. Social and economic interactions between countries throughout the world are known as

    A. synergy

    B. dependency

    C. globalization

    D. economic development

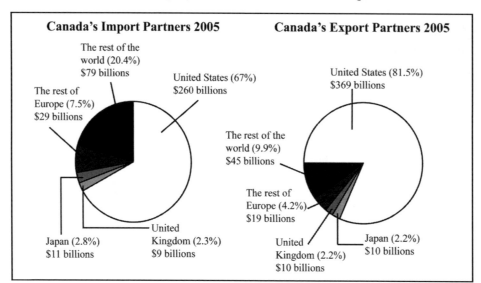

Use the following information to answer the next question.

11. Based on the given pie graphs, which of the following countries should Canada try to export more goods to in order to realize the greatest shift in the balance of trade in Canada's favour?

A. Japan

B. United Kingdom

C. The United States

D. The rest of the European countries

12. Generally, when an economic downturn is experienced within a country, the tourist industry in that country usually

A. falters, but more people travel within the country than abroad

B. improves as more people travel in that country and abroad

C. improves as more people travel domestically

D. falters and more people travel abroad

13. Kam and his family decided to visit a location in Canada that contains one of the tallest free-standing structures in the world. Which of the following cities did Kam and his family visit?

A. Niagara Falls

B. Quebec City

C. Montreal

D. Toronto

14. All of the following activities will contribute toward lowering Canadians' ecological footprints **except** for

    A. using solar energy

    B. throwing out broken items

    C. buying second-hand items

    D. eating leftovers from the day before

Use the following information to answer the next question.

The Spirit Bear is a rare, white-coloured species of bear that lives in rain forests along the coast of British Columbia. After ten years of citizen protest, plans were announced by the government of British Columbia in 2006 to protect 1.8 million hectares of land in the Great Bear Rainforest from logging operations.

15. Which of the following steps was most likely of **greatest** importance to the government before they made their decision to set aside and protect the areas of rain forest for the Spirit Bears?

    A. Determining if the logging operations could still make a profit without the forested lands

    B. Having an environmental assessment done to study habitat concerns

    C. Gathering information from a variety of secondary sources

    D. Allowing public input into the process

16. What is "green-washing"?

    A. Using natural, environmentally friendly substances to clean fruit

    B. Failing to prevent fertilizers from washing into nearby rivers and lakes

    C. Hiding environmental abuses behind a public façade of environmentalism

    D. Suddenly and rapidly changing business practices to become environmentally friendly

17. What characterizes a fair-trade product?

    A. No tariffs or duties were levied on the product.

    B. The product was produced in an environmentally safe manner.

    C. Plantation owners, shippers, and sellers all received a fair price for the product.

    D. Plantation workers received a fair wage for their labour to produce the product.

18. What is leachate?

    A. An organic fertilizer

    B. A controversial pesticide

    C. Toxic ash from incinerators

    D. Contaminated water from landfills

19. What is the **primary** pollutant produced by modern incinerators?

    A. Toxic ash

    B. Fine particles

    C. Greenhouse gases

    D. Dioxins and furans

20. What process uses superheated gases to destroy waste?

    A. Thermal treatment

    B. Plasma arc gasification

    C. Thermal depolymerization

    D. Mechanical biological treatment

21. Which greenhouse gas is **strongly** linked to Earth's mean temperature?

    A. Methane

    B. Nitrous oxide

    C. Carbon dioxide

    D. Chlorofluorocarbon

22. Which of the following problems would **not** occur as a result of global warming?

    A. Lower sea levels

    B. More extreme weather

    C. Spread of tropical diseases

    D. Extinction of plants and animals

23. Bands of land that exist between two or more ecozones and contain the combined features of those zones are best known as

    A. biomes

    B. ecumenes

    C. boundaries

    D. transitional zones

24. The Boreal Forest biome that exists in Canada also exists in the northern part of

    A. Asia

    B. Africa

    C. Australia

    D. South America

25. The **main** reason that earthquakes do not occur more often is that
    A. earthquakes take time to build up
    B. the crustal plates of the lithosphere move very slowly
    C. earthquakes are dependent on global seasonal climate
    D. the atmosphere influences activity within the lithosphere

26. Which of the following human systems did settlers **most likely** depend on in order to move westward and settle in the Prairie region of Canada?
    A. Communication systems
    B. Transportation systems
    C. Infrastructure systems
    D. Energy systems

27. Reducing the use of wood and paper products in Canada would have the **greatest** impact on resource-based industry that is carried out in which of the following Canadian ecozones?
    A. Mixedwood Plains
    B. Arctic Cordillera
    C. Boreal Shield
    D. Pacific

28. Neighbouring satellite communities have built up next to major cities **mainly** in response to
    A. agricultural activities
    B. transportation systems
    C. manufacturing activities
    D. primary resource development

29. The location of which of the following types of industries is **most** dependent upon its surrounding geography?
    A. Primary
    B. Secondary
    C. Tertiary
    D. Quaternary

Use the following information to answer the next question.

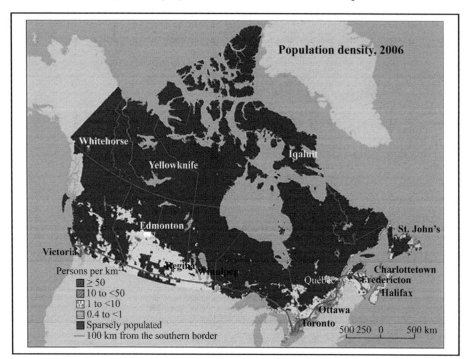

30. Upon observing the given map, which of the following reasons **most likely** explains why central Manitoba has a significantly lower population than central Alberta and central Saskatchewan?

A. The land in central Manitoba has less resource-based activity.

B. The majority of Manitoba's population is based around the provincial capital of Winnipeg.

C. Manitoba's population is located close to the American border in order to be close to trading activity.

D. People prefer the climate in central Alberta and central Saskatchewan more than that of central Manitoba.

31. Historically, the **main** type of economic activity that the Métis community in western Canada took part in was

A. mining

B. fishing

C. hunting

D. farming

32. All of the following terms were included in the Nunavut comprehensive land claim **except** for

A. $1.1 billion over time to benefit the people, ecosystem, and the economy

B. protected areas for a number of Arctic bioregions

C. all mineral rights to the land

D. additional parks

33. The emergence of smart growth plans that try to develop compact communities of people would strive toward controlling or eliminating all of the following conditions **except**

    A. urban sprawl

    B. urban congestion

    C. resource development

    D. resource sustainability

34. During times of extreme weather, which of the following services would be of **greatest** immediate importance to the residents of Nunavut?

    A. Communications services

    B. Transportation services

    C. Infrastructure services

    D. Recreational services

35. In which of the following ecozones would new immigrants to Canada **most likely** choose to live?

    A. Montane Cordillera

    B. Mixedwood Plains

    C. Atlantic Maritime

    D. Prairies

36. In order to lower greenhouse gas emissions, future locations of industries and transportation systems in Canada will **most likely** need to be built in locations with good access to

    A. primary natural resources

    B. renewable energy sources

    C. quaternary industries

    D. workers

37. Aboriginal artists often use which of the following art forms to create lifelike and three-dimensional works that demonstrate a strong connection to and respect for nature and animals?

    A. Woodburning

    B. Weaving

    C. Painting

    D. Carving

38. Which of the following consequences does **not** result from the clear-cutting of forests?

    A. Soil erosion

    B. Barren conditions

    C. Elimination of wildlife habitat

    D. Increase in biodiversity of the area

39. Which of the following Ontario environmental initiatives served as a model to city governments throughout North America?

    A. Creating compact communities

    B. Green space planning

    C. Blue box recycling

    D. Forest harvesting

40. The **main** reason that bees are extremely important to the agricultural industry is that

    A. honey sales are economically profitable to the industry

    B. bees control the number of insects that can harm crop growth

    C. animals that eat and destroy fruit crops are scared away by bees

    D. bees are involved in pollinating many of the natural foods that people eat

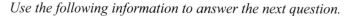

Use the following information to answer the next question.

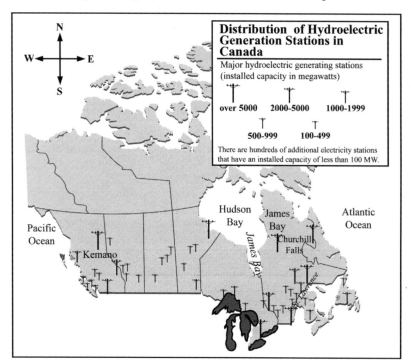

41. Upon studying the given map, which of the following provinces would gain the **most** economic benefit from hydroelectric generation?

    A. Quebec

    B. Alberta

    C. Ontario

    D. British Columbia

42. In recent years, the government has taken measures to promote the combined use of which of the following energy sources with a type of traditional energy source?

    A. Hydroelectricity

    B. Fuel minerals

    C. Wind energy

    D. Biofuels

43. Centuries ago, traditional ecological knowledge (TEK) helped Aboriginal peoples to understand all of the following environmental topics **except**

    A. the relationship between people and the environment

    B. the cyclical nature of natural systems

    C. interacting global climate systems

    D. resource sustainability

44. Which of the following actions is **most likely** of greatest potential damage to agricultural lands?

    A. Pesticide use

    B. Crop rotation

    C. High-yield seeds

    D. The building of shelterbelts

45. Resource depletion within one of Canada's valuable resource-based industries has led to which of the following initiatives?

    A. The use of irrigation in farming

    B. The development of aquaculture

    C. Cubic zirconium jewellery production

    D. Increased use of metal in furniture-making

46. Which of the following renewable or alternative energy sources has **most likely** encountered some environmental concern over the amount of land required to create it?

    A. Hydrogen fuel cells

    B. Wind energy

    C. Solar energy

    D. Ethanol

47. Damage to waterfowl has been of particular concern during the operation of which of the following resource megaprojects?

A. Athabasca oilsands

B. Hibernia offshore oil field

C. James Bay hydro complex

D. Northwest Territories diamond mines

48. Which of the following areas, which have often been encroached upon by urban sprawl and economic development, **most likely** supported the greatest amount of environmental biodiversity?

A. Mountain meadowlands

B. Prime agricultural lands

C. Green belts

D. Wetlands

49. Researching ways to improve the balance between human and natural systems involves all of the following topics **except**

A. ecologically restoring urban areas

B. lowering industrial pollution levels

C. increasing peoples' ecological footprints

D. developing waste management strategies

50. Future compact urban communities would seek waste management methods that meet all of the following criteria **except**

A. demonstrating economic feasibility

B. promoting resource conservation

C. meeting community approval

D. developing green space areas

51. Sustainable resource use in the Mixedwood Plains ecozone would involve all of the following activities **except**

A. running some public transportation on energy created by hydrogen fuel cells

B. converting wetlands to areas of agricultural development

C. using renewable energy sources to power machines

D. recycling waste products

52. All of the following activities would contribute to the quality of life for many Canadians nationwide **except**

  A. encouraging industries to use renewable energy sources

  B. purchasing rechargeable batteries for devices

  C. using organic cleaning supplies

  D. utilizing tidal energy

Practice Test

ANSWERS AND SOLUTIONS—PRACTICE TEST

1. B	12. A	23. D	34. A	45. B
2. D	13. D	24. A	35. B	46. D
3. D	14. B	25. B	36. B	47. A
4. A	15. B	26. B	37. D	48. D
5. C	16. C	27. C	38. D	49. C
6. A	17. D	28. C	39. C	50. D
7. A	18. D	29. A	40. D	51. B
8. D	19. A	30. A	41. A	52. D
9. D	20. B	31. C	42. D	
10. C	21. C	32. C	43. C	
11. D	22. A	33. D	44. A	

1. B

The World Trade Organization, not the United Nations, develops and overseas guidelines concerning international trade.

The United Nations provides assistance to countries during times of international need, such as following a natural disaster. The United Nations' goals include providing support for human rights—Canada's early participation in the United Nations included the drafting of the Universal Declaration of Human Rights. The United Nations Environment Programme is actively involved in addressing environmental issues affecting Earth.

2. D

The goals of the Asia-Pacific Economic Cooperation (APEC) include promoting free trade and economic growth among 21 member countries on four continents. The geographic area encompassed by APEC countries includes approximately 50% of the global population. Canada's greatest opportunity to gain overseas trading partners most likely occurs through its participation in APEC initiatives.

NAFTA is a North American trading agreement involving Canada, Mexico, and the United States. It is not as likely to garner overseas trading partners for Canada. The United Nations was formed with the intent to promote peace, cooperation, and security throughout the world. It is not as likely to garner overseas trading partners for Canada. The World Trade Organization is an international organization that oversees guidelines concerning international trade. Canada's involvement with this group may gain overseas trading alliances, but probably not to the extent of Canada's membership and participation in the Asia-Pacific Economic Cooperation.

3. D

CIDA was formed primarily to help people in the world who have suffered hardships and require humanitarian aid and sustainable development of their environment. Needing to address energy issues would not involve the primary efforts of CIDA.

The Canadian International Development Agency was established by the Canadian government primarily to help people in regions of the world that have suffered hardships such as disease, famine, conflict, or natural disaster. Running out of natural resources may contribute to these hardships.

4. A

The location of Earth's global biomes is strongly related to where particular climate patterns exist.

The location of Earth's ecosystems is not related to where particular tectonic plates exist. The location of Earth's crustal plates is not related to where particular human systems exist. The location of the Ring of Fire is not related to where particular global biomes exist.

5. C

The location of the continents is not a major contributor to the formation of Earth's global climate system.

The influences of the atmosphere, the circulation of ocean waters, and the differences in landforms are major contributors to the formation of Earth's global climate system.

6. A

Some environmentalists feel that twenty years is not long enough to complete some stages of forestry activity and for areas of forest to be replanted and grow on their own successfully.

The fact that a political party could change power may not necessarily be a major issue, as forestry companies would need to follow the original plans. New and environmentally friendly technologies in forest harvesting can most likely be used by forestry companies regardless of the time period addressed in a forestry plan. One-year forestry plans would not be practical and may not sufficiently address long-term goals.

7. A

Freezing rain does not involve the depletion of Canada's natural resources.

Government measures to ensure the responsible use of pesticides would benefit Canadian soils (natural resources) and human health. Government measures to address deforestation would benefit Canada's forests. Government measures to address cross-border pollution would benefit Canada's water supply.

8. D

The decline of fish stocks is a concern to some countries—for example, Canada. This concern is more localized to individual countries as opposed to being an issue of global magnitude.

The protection of human rights, deforestation, and global warming are global issues.

9. D

Canada is a very large country, and geographic considerations make it more economical to import oil to some locations in Canada rather than transporting it across the country. It can be cheaper to transport oil south to American markets, thus making it more economical to import some Canadian requirements.

Canada does not require a higher grade of oil. Costs involved in washing oil out of the oil sands is not the reason why Canada imports oil. Canada has adequate economic funds to produce oil.

10. C

Social and economic interactions between countries throughout the world are known as globalization.

In natural systems, synergy describes the total effect of two or more systems that, when working together, produce an effect larger than what could be produced from each system on its own. Dependency is when one country is dependent on another. Economic development is growth within a particular country related to the country's production of goods and services.

11. D

Canada does not have a favorable balance of trade with the other combined European countries besides the United Kingdom—for example, only $19 billion in Canadian goods and services were exported to the other European countries in comparison to $29 billion in other European countries' goods and services that were imported to Canada. In terms of the balance of trade concerning the given alternatives, the greatest shift in gains would be realized by Canada exporting more goods to the other European countries.

Canada had a comparatively closer balance of trade with Japan than the other European countries—for example, $10 billion in Canadian goods and services were exported to Japan and $11 billion in goods and services were imported from Japan. Canada had a slightly favourable balance of trade with the United Kingdom—for example, $10 billion in Canadian goods and services were exported to the United Kingdom and $9 billion in United Kingdom goods and services were imported to Canada. Canada had a favourable balance of trade with the United States—for example, $369 billion in Canadian goods and services were exported to the United States and $260 billion in American goods and services were imported to Canada.

12. A

Usually, the tourist industry will falter in an economic downturn, but those who travel will tend to travel domestically (within the country) more frequently than abroad because of the expenses involved in international travel. Usually, the tourist industry will also falter because of diminished funds of potential travelers or a trend not to spend their funds as a result of job security and economic decline.

13. D

Kam and his family visited Toronto. The CN Tower is one of the tallest free-standing structures in the world.

14. B

Broken items can often be fixed and reused, which will contribute toward lowering Canadians' ecological footprints.

Using solar energy, buying second-hand items, and eating healthy leftovers from the day before instead of preparing and using more food will contribute toward lowering Canadians' ecological footprints.

15. B

Having an environmental assessment done to study the habitat concerns of the Spirit Bear would be of great significance to the government in order to learn firsthand whether this species could exist under current environmental circumstances. In addressing this environmental issue, the government would most likely want to thoroughly assess the habitat concerns of the Spirit Bear versus the interests of the logging companies.

Secondary sources include journals, books, and documentaries. Primary sources such as the opinion of habitat experts or an environmental assessment would be sources of firsthand knowledge to the government and other concerned groups. Allowing public input into the process would be very important, but having firsthand habitat information concerning the consequences to the Spirit Bears' local ecosystem as a result of logging operations would provide the government with valuable information in determining a solution to this environmental issue.

16. C

Because consumers are increasingly concerned about the environment, many choose to consume products that are produced in an ecologically sound manner. This has prompted many companies, regardless of their actual environmental practices, to "green-wash" their image; that is, they advertise themselves as environmentally friendly, even if they are not, in order to attract consumers.

17. D

Fair-trade products are those that are produced in a socially ethical manner; in other words, the workers had safe working conditions, were compensated fairly, and so forth.

18. D

Leachate is water that percolates through landfill trash. If the landfill does not have a lining or if the lining is breached, this contaminated water can leak through the soil and enter ground water.

19. A

After incineration there remains a significant level of ash. This ash tends to be laden with heavy metals and other potentially toxic substances.

Fine particles, greenhouse gases, and dioxins and furans are all pollutants generated by early incinerators; however, these pollutants are strictly controlled in modern incinerators.

20. B

Plasma arc gasification occurs when inert gases are vented through a strong electrical arc. The gases become superheated and can break waste down into its component elements.

Thermal treatment is another term for incineration. Thermal depolymerization is the use of steam to convert plastics and biomass (e.g., waste of biological origin) into light crude oil. Mechanical biological treatment uses natural decomposition processes to treat biological waste—it is similar to composting.

21. C

Although carbon dioxide is the weakest of the greenhouse gases listed, it is the most abundant. Scientists have linked Earth's mean temperature over hundreds of thousands of years to the amount of carbon dioxide in the atmosphere.

22. A

Because of melting ice in the polar regions, the sea level would actually rise as a result of global warming.

23. D

Transitional zones are boundaries through which the features of one ecozone gradually blend in a transitional area with characteristics of the next ecozone.

Biomes are large ecological areas on Earth that are named after the distinct characteristics of the plants living within them. An ecumene refers to an inhabited area of the world. Boundaries are natural lines, or borders, that separate one region from another. The tree line is an example of a boundary.

24. A

The Boreal Forest biome also exists in northern Asia—for example, Russia. The worldwide location of biomes and the unique vegetation that grows within them corresponds to common zones of latitude in which biomes exist worldwide. The Boreal Forest biome does not exist in the northern parts of Africa, Australia, or South America.

25. B

The main reason that earthquakes do not occur more often is because earthquakes occur as a result of the movement of crustal plates, and this movement is very slow.

Earthquakes build up over time as a result of the slow movement of Earth's crustal plates. The influence of the atmosphere upon the lithosphere is not the reason why earthquakes occur when they do. Earthquakes are not dependent upon global seasonal climate.

26. B

Settlers depended heavily on transportation systems. Transportation systems, which at that time consisted primarily of waterways and paths for horses and wagons, were key to settlers being able to travel across the country.

Communication systems were very basic and scarce at that time. Infrastructure networks, which communities depend upon to provide people with basic services, did not exist prior to settlement and the advance of more modern technologies. Energy networks that collect, transport, and deliver sources of energy to people did not exist prior to settlement and the advance of more modern technologies.

27. C

The Boreal Shield ecozone would be most impacted by the reduction of the use of wood and paper products in Canada, as forestry is a major primary industry that is located there.

The Mixedwood Plains consists of flat lands with fertile soils. Agriculture is a resource-based industry in the Mixedwood Plains ecozone. The Arctic Cordillera would not support a forestry industry. The Pacific ecozone is a marine ecozone located off the coast of British Columbia.

28. C

Neighboring satellite communities have built up next to major cities primarily in response to the need for labour and services to support the manufacturing industries within those cities.

A satellite community would not likely build up next to a major city in response to agricultural activities. Neighbouring satellite communities have not built up next to major cities in response to transportation systems, as there would be other factors necessary, such as employment, to influence the growth of these communities. Primary resource development (forestry, mining, etc.) takes place in rural areas.

29. A

The location of primary industries is most dependent on their surrounding geography, as primary resources must be derived or harvested from the natural environment. For example, the mining industry is dependent on being based in a location that has minerals that can be mined.

Secondary industry, such as manufacturing, is not as dependent on its surrounding geographic location as primary industry. Tertiary industry, or the service industry, is not as dependent on its surrounding geographic location as primary industry. Quaternary industry, which involves the creation of knowledge, technology, and ideas in order to create solutions, is not as dependent on its surrounding geographic location as primary industry.

30. A

A hypothesis can be made that some types of resource-based activities do not exist in central Manitoba that do exist in central Saskatchewan and central Alberta because central Manitoba is covered by the Canadian Shield. For example, agriculture is much stronger in central Alberta and central Saskatchewan where the land is more fertile.

The majority of Manitoba's population is based in southern Manitoba, not just around Winnipeg. The area of western Ontario adjacent to southern Manitoba is scarce in its population, yet it is also very close to the American border. Therefore, being close to the American border cannot be the primary reason that the majority of Manitoba's population lives in southern Manitoba. The climate in central Manitoba is very similar to the climate in central Alberta and central Saskatchewan.

31. C

The Métis are descendants of Aboriginal peoples and early European fur traders. Historically, the Métis community that formed in western Canada was very involved in the fur trade. Some Métis, however, did farm and fish.

Mining and fishing were not the main types of economic activities that the Métis took part in. Many Métis farmed, but hunting and trapping were the main types of economic activities that the Métis took part in.

32. C

Mineral rights to 10% of the land were granted, not all mineral rights, with the remaining resources shared with the government.

The amount of $1.1 billion over time to benefit the people, ecosystem, and the economy was granted. Protected areas were to be set aside for 24 Arctic bioregions. Additional parks were granted as part of the comprehensive land claim.

33. D

Smart growth urban plans aim toward encouraging resource sustainability.

Smart growth urban plans would aim toward controlling or eliminating urban sprawl, urban congestion, and resource development.

34. A

Communications services would be of the greatest immediate importance in terms of obtaining and ensuring help for people.

Transportation and infrastructure services would be of great importance, but communications services would most likely be of the greatest immediate importance. Recreational services would not be of importance.

35. B

The majority of immigrants who move to Canada choose to live in Toronto (43%), Montreal, and Vancouver, often for employment opportunities that exist and cultural connections within the cities. Thus, new immigrants to Canada would most likely choose to live in the Mixedwood Plains ecozone.

36. B

Having renewable energy sources nearby will provide industries with clean energy and reduce greenhouse gas emissions.

Having primary resources nearby (e.g., those that are derived from the ground or harvested like minerals or crops) would not cause industries to have lower emissions. Having quaternary industries nearby (those that produce knowledge, ideas, and technology to create solutions to problems) would not contribute to lower greenhouse gas emissions. Having a good supply of workers nearby would not cause an industry to have lower greenhouse gas emissions.

37. D

Carving is the art form that Aboriginal artists often use to create lifelike and three-dimensional works that demonstrate a strong connection to and respect for nature.

Woodburning, weaving, and painting are not art forms that Aboriginal artists often use to create lifelike and three-dimensional works that demonstrate a strong connection to and respect for nature.

38. D

Clear-cutting often leads to a loss of biodiversity in areas where it occurs.

Clear-cutting often leads to soil erosion, a barren, desert-like appearance, and the elimination of wildlife habitats in an area following the removal of all of the trees.

39. C

Ontario's blue box program served as an environmental waste management model to city governments throughout North America.

Ontario has plans for creating compact communities. Ontario has set aside many areas for green space. Forest harvesting is not an environmental initiative.

40. D

Bees, butterflies, and birds play an important role in pollinating at least one-third of the foods that people eat in Canada.

Though honey sales may be profitable, the main reason that bees are important to the agricultural industry is that they play an important role in pollinating crops.

41. A

According to the given map, there are more hydroelectric stations in Quebec than the other provinces. The more hydroelectricity that can be sold, the greater the economic gain.

Quebec would most likely gain more economic benefit from hydroelectric generation than Alberta, Ontario, and British Columbia, as it has more generating hydroelectric stations.

42. D

Planned regulations seek a 5% renewable content of gasoline by ethanol. The government sought this change in order to promote a sustainable environment.

43. C

Centuries ago, Aboriginal peoples would have experienced the effects of those climate systems that affected the areas in which they lived. They would not have experienced the interactions of the many global climate systems that occur throughout the world.

TEK would have helped Aboriginal peoples to understand the relationship between people and the environment, the cyclical nature of natural systems, and resource sustainability. Aboriginal peoples have a deep respect for and close relationship with nature. Resources such as animals, trees, and vegetation would have been used with great respect for the sustainability of their natural systems.

44. A

Pesticide use can be damaging to the soils in which crops grow, and they can be potentially damaging to the health of humans, animals, and vegetation.

Crop rotation serves to revive soils and promote their productivity. High-yield seeds increase the amount of food that agricultural lands can produce. Building a shelterbelt around a farm serves to protect the soil from erosion.

45. B

Aquaculture, or fish farming, has developed in Canada in response to the serious depletion of Canada's fishing stocks. Fishing was once a major resource-based industry in Canada.

46. D

Acres of farmland must be utilized to grow the corn to make ethanol. This can disrupt the ecosystems of animals and plants and has sometimes been brought up as a concern.

Wind turbines do not require as much land space as growing corn for ethanol. Solar power and hydrogen fuel cells do not require acres of land to create their energy.

47. A

Waterfowl that exist near the Athabasca oilsands have at times found it difficult to fly because of oil that was stuck in their feathers, and birds have occasionally been poisoned by the oil.

48. D

Wetlands are areas of vast ecological biodiversity that are home to many species of insects, fish, reptiles, birds, plants, and other living organisms.

Mountain meadowlands would not as likely be locations of urban sprawl and economic development. Prime agricultural lands would not necessarily have had the extent of biodiversity as areas of marshland. Greenbelts may contain varying amounts of biodiversity depending upon their location.

49. C

Researching ways to improve the balance between human and natural systems would likely involve ways to lower peoples' ecological footprints, not increase them.

Researching ways to improve the balance between human and natural systems would likely involve the topic of lowering industrial pollution levels, ecologically restoring urban areas, and developing waste management strategies.

50. D

Future urban communities will most likely not develop green space areas, as these areas have been set aside for the preservation and protection of natural ecosystems.

Future urban communities will most likely seek waste management methods that are economically feasible, promote resource conservation and a sustainable environment, and meet the approval of community members.

51. B

Wetlands are valuable ecological areas, and more than 90% of wetland areas in the Mixedwood Plains ecozone have already experienced drainage to accommodate agriculture or urban development. Sustainable resource use would most likely not involve this type of activity.

Using renewable energy sources to power machines and recycling products would promote the sustainability of resources.

52. D

Utilizing tidal energy may not contribute to the quality of life for large numbers of Canadians nationwide, as the geographic circumstances necessary to create tidal energy are limiting to its availability.

Encouraging industries to use renewable energy sources would reduce emissions into the environment. Using rechargeable batteries for devices cuts down on the need to purchase new batteries and for new batteries to be produced. Organic cleaning supplies are those made of natural ingredients. Using organic cleaning supplies can benefit the health of many Canadians. For example, a number of people have sensitivities to the chemicals contained in some cleaning supplies.

NOTES

Appendices

GLOSSARY

Asian-Pacific Economic Cooperation (APEC)	An intergovernmental forum that promotes free trade, cooperation, and economic growth in the Asia-Pacific region.
atmosphere	The thin layer of odourless, colourless, and tasteless gases surrounding Earth.
biofuel	Cleaner, renewable fuel types
biomes	Large ecological regions on Earth that are named after the distinct characteristics of the plants living within them.
bioregion	A localized area with unique natural characteristics such as climate, landforms, soils, plants, and animals.
boundaries	Natural lines or borders that separate one region from another.
Canadian International Development Agency (CIDA)	An agency established to help people in regions of the world who have suffered hardships, such as disease and famine.
climate	The average pattern of weather that has existed in a particular region over many years.
commercial lands	Used for business activities that provide goods and services to people; for example, a shopping mall.
communication systems	All types of communication, such as telephone and e-mail networks, that enable people to be connected to each other.
comprehensive land claims	Aboriginal claims to land, self-governance, and natural resources in areas where treaties have never existed.
demography	The study of population statistics
ecological footprint	A measurement in hectares that calculates the amount of land and resources required to support the lifestyle of a country or an individual.
economic immigration	When people come to Canada to work
economic systems	Coordinated and combined activities that enable goods and services to be produced and delivered.
ecosystem	A community of animals and plants that interact with their environment.
ecozone	A vast region comprising a combination of interacting human and natural characteristics.
ecumene	Inhabited area of the world.
energy networks	To provide the energy necessary to support the Canadian lifestyle
globalization	The forming of global relationships from increasing economic and social interactions among countries throughout the world.
hydrosphere	Includes all forms of water on Earth's crust (solid, liquid, and gas).
incinerators	Facilities where waste is burned at very high temperatures.
industrial lands	Lands used to support secondary industries; for example, factories.

infrastructure system	The networks of basic services that communities and economies need in order to function successfully.
institutional lands	Lands used for services provided to communities; for example, schools.
Kyoto Protocol	An agreement designed to limit energy emissions and the production of greenhouse gases that occur in the atmosphere as a result of emissions, much of it produced by industries and automobile use.
La Francophonie	A global organization that Canada participates in to support the role of its Francophone community internationally. It serves to promote linguistic and cultural diversity, peace, human rights, democracy, education and research, and cooperation toward sustainable development.
landfill	Sites where trash is delivered, compacted, and stored, generally in large pits.
lithosphere	Earth's outer layer, which includes all of Earth's crust and the top part of its mantle.
muskeg	Areas of wetland bogs of decayed vegetation.
North American Free Trade Agreement (NAFTA)	A free trade agreement that was signed by Canada, the United States, and Mexico in 1992, thus forming the world's largest free trade area.
open space lands	Unused and protected lands as well as lands used for recreation.
passive solar power	Occurs when the sun enters through windows. Heat is absorbed into walls, floors, and furniture and is radiated back as heat energy.
physical processes	Processes that occur gradually over time, such as erosion and weathering.
plasma arc gasification	Inert gases are vented through a powerful electrical arc to break down waste into component elements.
plate tectonics	This process forms mountains that exist in Canada and throughout the world.
population density	How heavily an area is populated; how crowded an area is.
primary industries	Industries based on the extraction of natural resources, such as mining, forestry, and fishing.
...ll factors	Factors that encourage people to emigrate to a particular nation
...ctors	Factors that encourage people to decide to leave a particular nation.
...ndustries	Industries involving the formation of knowledge, technology, and ideas in order to create solutions to problems.
	Lands used for leisure and sporting activities.
	People who have had to flee their home nation because they are in danger.
	...used for living space.
	...f earthquakes and volcanic activity that occurs around the edge of the
	...xists outside of towns and cities where the land has a low
	...tput of primary industries and turn them into
	...o the future.
	...ow the different parts of the environment fit together into ...ems.

tertiary industries	Service-based industries, such as health care and finance.
transition zone	A boundary through which the features of one ecozone gradually blend in a transitional area with characteristics of the next ecozone.
transportation lands	Lands used for transportation routes that move people and goods from place to place; for example, highways.
transportation systems	Interconnected networks of roads and routes designed to easily move people and all kinds of goods across Canada (rail, bus, bicycle, air, and waterways).
United Nations (UN)	An organization that was formed following the Second World War with the desire to create peace, cooperation, and security throughout the world.
urban environment	A centre of human settlement and activity that has acquired a large population density.
urban sprawl	Occurs as a result of the outward expansion and development of urban areas to nearby bordering areas.
watershed	Drains rain or snowfall toward a particular waterway.
World Trade Organization	A group that develops and oversees guidelines concerning international trade.

CREDITS

Every effort has been made to provide proper acknowledgement of the original source and to comply with copyright law. However, some attempts to establish original copyright ownership may have been unsuccessful. If copyright ownership can be identified, please notify Castle Rock Research Corp so that appropriate corrective action can be taken.

Some images in this document are from www.clipart.com, © 2013 Clipart.com, a division of Getty Images.

Map: Canadian Population Density Map, 2006, from Statistics Canada. http://www12.statcan.ca/english/census06/analysis/popdwell/vignettes/map-2006-pop-dnesity-canada-sz02-en.htm.

Graph: Proportion of the Canadian Population Living in Urban Regions since 1901, from Statistics Canada

Graph: Percentage change in Rural and Urban population in Canada from 1971 to 2001, adapted from Statistics Canada

Chart: Canada's Import and Export Partners 2005 adapted from Statistics Canada. From "Encounter Canada: Land, People, Environment" by Patricia Healy, et al. © 2007 Oxford University Press

Statistics Canada information is used with the permission of Statistics Canada. Users are forbidden to copy this material and/or re-disseminate the data, in an original or modified form, for commercial purposes without the expressed permission of Statistics Canada. Information on the availability of the wide range of data from Statistics Canada can be obtained from Statistics Canada's Regional Offices, its World Wide Web site at http://www.statcan.ca, and its toll-free access number 1-800-263-1136.

NOTES

NOTES

NOTES

NOTES

NOTES

NOTES

NOTES

SOLARO Study Guides
Ordering Information

SOLARO
Study Guides

The SOLARO Study Guides are specifically designed to assist students in preparing for unit tests, final exams, and provincial assessments.

SOLARO Study Guide—$29.95 each plus applicable sales tax

Ontario SOLARO Titles	
Mathematics 12, Advanced Functions, University Prep (MHF4U)	Civics 10, (CHV2O)
Mathematics 12, Calculus and Vectors, University Prep (MCV4U)	English 10, Academic (ENG2D)
Mathematics 12, Mathematics of Data Management, University Prep (MDM4U)	OSSLT, Ontario Secondary School Literacy Test
Physics 12, University Prep (SPH4U)	Mathematics 9, Academic, Principles of Mathematics (MPM1D)
Biology 12, University Prep (SBI4U)	Mathematics 9, Applied, Foundations of Mathematics (MFM1P)
Canadian and World Politics 12, University Prep (CPW4U)	Science 9, Academic (SNC1D)
Chemistry 12, University Prep (SCH4U)	Science 9, Applied (SNC2P)
English 12, University Prep (ENG4U)	Geography of Canada 9, Academic (CGC1D)
English 12, College Prep (ENG4C)	English 9, Academic (ENG1D)
World History 12, University Prep (CHY4U)	Science 8
Mathematics 11, Foundations for College Mathematics (MBF3C)	Mathematics 7
Mathematics 11, Functions and Applications, U/C Prep (MCF3M)	Science 7
Mathematics 11, Functions, University Prep (MCR3U)	Mathematics 6
Biology 11, University Prep (SBI3U)	Science 6
Chemistry 11, University Prep (SCH3U)	Language 6
English 11, University Prep (ENG3U)	Mathematics 5
World History 11, University/College Prep (CHW3M)	Science 5
Mathematics 10, Academic, Principles of Mathematics (MPM2D)	Mathematics 4
Mathematics 10, Applied, Foundations of Mathematics (MFM2P)	Science 4
Science 10, Applied (SNC1P)	Mathematics 3
Science 10, Academic (SNC2D)	Science 3
Canadian History 10, Academic (CHC2D)	Language 3
Canadian History 10, Applied (CHC2P)	

To order books, please visit
castlerockresearch.com or call
1.800.840.6224
Volume pricing is available. Contact us at
orders@castlerockresearch.com

Student Notes and Problems
Workbook
Ordering Information

Student Notes and Problems (SNAP) Workbooks contain complete explanations of curriculum concepts, including examples and practice exercises

SNAP Workbook—$29.95 each plus applicable sales tax

Ontario SNAP Titles
Physics 12, University Preparation (SPH4U)
Physics 11, University Preparation (SPH3U)
Math 10, Academic, Principles of Mathematics (MPM2D)
Math 9, Academic, Principles of Mathematics (MPM1D)
Math 9, Applied, Foundations of Mathematics (MFM1P)

Total Cost

SOLARO Study Guides Ordered _____

SNAP Books Ordered _____

Cost Subtotal _____

Shipping and Handling
Please call for current rates _____

GST _____

Order Total _____

Payment and Shipping Information

Name _____

School _____

Telephone _____

SHIP TO:

School Code _____

School Name _____

Address _____

City: _____

Postal Code: _____

PAYMENT OPTIONS:

☐ By Credit Care VISA/MC

Name on Card: _____

Number: _____

Expirely Date: _____

☐ By Enclosed Cheque

☐ Invoice School

PO Number: _____

To order books, please visit
www.castlerockresearch.com

Volume pricing is available. Contact us at
orders@castlerockresearch.com